The History
of
Pleasant Valley, New York

Cover picture: The covered bridge over the Wappingers Creek. You would see this bridge as you entered town from the east in 1908. A drawing of this bridge is on the town seal.

The History of Pleasant Valley, New York

By Pat Holt

All rights reserved. No parts of this book may be used or reproduced in any manner whatsoever without written permission, except in case of brief quotations embodied in critical articles or reviews.

Copyright © 2012 Pat Holt All rights reserved

Second Edition

Burr Oak Publishing
www.burroakpublishing.com

Printed in the U.S.A.

I would like to express my appreciation to the following individuals and organizations for their invaluable help in making this book possible: Marcia Johnson Valdata, Patricia Silvernail Beatty, Barbara Germiller Herles for their quick response to my email questions about the history of our generation in Pleasant Valley. Caroline Dolfi, Pam Cady, Fred Schaefer for pictures. George Greenwood for organizing digital images on the computer, Terri Ghee, Charlotte Jones and Kay Mackey, the volunteers at the office of the Town Historian at the Mill Site Museum. Teddi Luzzi Southworth for her current Pleasant Valley photos and her willingness to take more when needed.

A special thanks to WOW (Winn's Orphan Writers) for their patience as I read and re-read stories of Pleasant Valley to them.

Special acknowledgement to Susan Holland, owner of the Country Thistle on Main Street in Pleasant Valley for her words that day that now seems so long ago, "Someone should write a book about the history of Pleasant Valley." To which I replied with my usual enthusiasm, "I could do that!" From there the journey to write this book began. Terri Ghee and I went to the Mill Site Museum office and started gathering information.

Table of Contents

Early Pleasant Valley

Following is a copy of the hand written Original Nine Partners Patent[1] that gave the area that became Dutchess County to the nine partners. Part of this area became Pleasant Valley in 1821.

Lewis A. Scott. Secretary.

Recorded for Coll Caleb Heathcote & Company -

William the third by the Grace of God King of England Scotland ffrance and Ireland Defender of the faith &c To all to whome these Presents shall come Sendeth Greeting Whereas our Loving Subjects Coll Caleb Heathcote one of our Council of our Province of New Yorke &c Major Augustine Graham James Emott Leiut Coll Henry Filkin David Jamison Henry Tenyck John Aretson William Creed and Jarvis Marshall have by their Peticon Presented unto our - Trusty and welbeloved Benjamin Fletcher our Captaine Generall and - Governour in Cheife of our said Province of New Yorke and Territoryes Depend- ing thereon in America &c Prayed our Grant and Confirmation of a Certaine Tract of Vacant Land Scituate lying and being on Hudsons River within our - Dutchesse County Bounded on the West by the said Hudsons River betweene the - Creeke Called by the Indians Aquasing and by the Christians the fish - Creeke at the Marked Trees of Pauling (including the said Creeke) and - the Land of Meyndert Harmense & Company then Bounded Southerly by the Land of the said Meyndert Harmense & Company so farr as their Bounds Goes then Westerly by the Land of said Harmense and Company untill a -
P.88 Southerly Line Runn soe farr South untill it Comes to the South side of a Certaine Meadow wherein there is a White Oak Tree marked with the Letters H.T. then Southerly by an East and West Line to the Division Line between this our Province and our Collony of Connecticutt and so Easterly by the - said Division Line and Northerly by the aforesaid fish Creeke as farr as -

(it)

[1] A grant made by a government that confers on an individual fee-simple title to public lands

it Goes and from the Head of the said Creeke by a Parallell Line to the South Bounds East and West Reaching the aforesaid Division Line] which Request we being willing to Grant Know Yee that of our Speciall Grace Certaine Know-ledge and meere motion We have Given Granted Ratifyed and Confirmed and by these Presents Do for us our Heirs and Successours Give Grant Ratifie and Con-firme unto our said Loving Subjects Caleb Heathcote, Augustine Graham, James Emott, Henry ffilkin, David Jamison, Henry Tenyck, John Aretson, William Creed and Jarvis Marshall all the aforerecited Certaine Tract of Vacant Land Scituate Lyeing and being within the Limites and Bounds afore-said together with all and Singular the Woods Underwoods Trees Timber feilds feedings Pastures Meadows Marshes Swamps Pools Ponds Waters Watercourses fish Creek and other Rivers Rivoletts Streams Runns Quarryes fishing fouling hunting and hawking Mines Mineralls (Silver and Gold Mines Excepted) and all other Profites benefites Priviledges Comodityes Advantages Royaltyes Hereditaments and Appurtenances whatsoever to the aforerecited Certaine Tract of Land within the Limites and Bounds aforesaid Belonging or in any wayes Appertaining To have and to hold all the aforerecited Tract of Land within the Limites and Bounds aforesaid together with all and Singular the Woods Underwoods Trees Timber feilds feedings Pastures Meadows Marshes Swamps Pools Ponds Waters Watercourses fish Creeke and other Rivers, Rivoletts Streams Runns Quarryes fishing fouling hunting and hawking Mines Mineralls (Silver and Gold Mines Excepted) and all other Profites benefites Priviledges Comodityes Advantages Royaltyes Hereditaments and Appurtenances whatso-ever to the aforerecited Certaine Tract of Land within the Limites and Bounds

P. 89 – aforesaid Belonging or in any ways Appertaining unto them the said Caleb Heathcote Augustine Graham James Emott Henry ffelkin David Jamison Henry Tenyck John Aretson William Creed and Jarvis Marshall their Heirs and Assignes to the Sole and only Propper use Benefite & behoofe of them the said Caleb Heathcote Augustine Graham James Emott Henry Filkin David Jamison Henry Tenyck John Aretsen William Creed and Jarvis Marshall their Heirs and Assignes forever without any Lett Hindrance or Molestation to be had or Reserved upon Pretence of Joynt Tennancy or Survivorship any thing Conteind in these Presents to the Contrary in any wayes Notwithstanding To be holden of us our Heirs and Successours in ffree and Comon Soccage as of our Mannour of East Greenwich in our County of Kent within our Realme of England Yeilding Rendring and Paying therefore Yearly and every Year forever unto us our Heirs and Successours on the feast Day of the Annunciation of our blessed Virgin Mary at our City of New Yorke the Yearly Rent of three Pounds Currant Money of our said Province in Lieu and Stead of all other Rents Services Dues Dutyes and Demands whatsoever for the said Tract of Land and Premisses In Testimony whereof We have Caused the Great Seale of our said Province to be hereunto affixed Witnesse our said Trusty and welbeloved Benjamin Fletcher Benjamin Fletcher our Captaine Generall and Governour in Cheife of our Province of New Yorke and the Territoryes and Tracts of Land Depending thereon in America and Vice Admirall of the same our Leiv.t and Commander in Cheife of the Militia and of all the forces by Sea and Land within our Colony of Connecticutt and of all the ffurts and Places of Strength within the Same in Councill at our ffort in New Yorke the twenty Seventh Day of May in the Ninth Year of our Reigne Annoq Domini 1697 Ben ffletcher By his Excellencyes Command David Jamison D Secry

I do hereby Certify the aforegoing to be a true Copy of the Original Record. Word by 28th line page 87 being obliterated and betweene interlined in its stead as in the said Record. Compared therewith By Me

Lewis A: Scott Secretary.

98 Recorded for the Church Wardens and Vestrymen of the Church of England as by Law Established of Trinity Church in New Yorke

Guilielmus Tertius Dei Gratia Angliæ Scotiæ ffranciæ et Hiberniæ Rex fidei Defensor &c To all to whom these Presents shall come Sendeth greeting Whereas by an Act of Assembly made in the fifth Year of our Reigne Entituled An Act for Setling a Ministry and Raising a Maintainance for them in the City of New Yorke Countys of Richmond Westchester and Queens County among other things therein Conteined it is Enacted that there shall be Called inducted and Established a Good Sufficient Protestant Minister to Officiate and have the Care of Souls within our said City of

It wasn't until 1737 that the Indian deed released the rights of the Indians from the land. This copy of the Indian deed is from the Dutchess County Historical Society Yearbook, 1923, page 29 - 32.

Deed of the Great Nine Partners

The following is a copy of the original Indian deed of the Great or Lower Nine Partners patent granted 27th May 1697 to Caleb Heathcote, Augustine Graham, James Emmot, John Aertson, Henry Filkins, Hendrick Ten Eyck, Jarvis Marshall, David Jamison and William Creed. The Indian deed releasing the rights of the Indians was not given until 1737 at which time all of the patentees except David Jamison were dead.

GEORGE S. VAN VLIET.

DEED

To all Christian People to whom these presents shall come, wee, the native Indian proprietors of Land in Dutche County, viz't, Acgans, Nimham, Ouracgacguis, Taquahamas, Seeck, Pecewyn, Mamany, Perpuwas, Sasaaacgua, Wasanamonrg, Arichapeckt, Narcarindt, Ayawatack, Sacayawa, Cekounamow, Seeck's son named Arye, Wappenas, Tintgeme, Naghcharent, Nonnaparee, Kindtquaw, Shawanachko, and Shawasquo and Tounis son of the said Shawask:

Whereas there was granted by patent under seal of the province of New York, bearing date the twenty-seventh day of May in the year sixteen hundred and ninety-seven, by Christian calculation, unto Colonel Caleb Heathcote, one of King William's Council for the province of New York, in America, in his lifetime, Major Augustus Graham in his lifetime, James Emott in his lifetime, Lieu't Colonel Henry Filkin in his lifetime, David Jamison, Henryck Teneyck in his lifetime, John Aertson in his lifetime, William Creed in his lifetime, and Jarvis Marshall in his lifetime, a certain tract of vacant land, situate and being on Hudson's river, between the creek called by the natives Aquasing, and by the Christians by Fish Creek, at the markt trees of Pawling (including the said Creek) and the land of Meyndert Harmense and Company; then bounded southerly by said Land of Harmense & Company so farr as their bounds runns; then westerly by said land of Harmense and Company until a southerly line run so farr south until it comes to the southside of a certain meadow wherein there is a white oak tree marked with the letters HT; then bounded southerly by an east and west line to the division line between this province of Newyork and Colony of Connecticuts, and so bounded easterly by the said division line & northerly by said Fish creek

29

as farr as it goes & from the head thereof by a paralell line to the south bounds, running east and west to the said division line, with ith hereditaments & appurtenances,—to hold unto them, the said Caleb Heathcote, Augustus Graham, James Emott, Henry Filkin, David Jamison, Henrydck Tenyck, John Aertson, William Creed, and Jarvis Marshall, their heirs and assigns, forever. NOW, know you, that wee, the native proprietors of said tract of land, for and in consideration of certain goods and merchandize, to us in hand paid or secured to be paid at & before the ensealing of this present writing, have given, granted, bargained, sold, released, and confirmed, and do by these presents give, grant, bargain, sell, release and con firm, unto the said David Jamison, the only surviving patentee of the said patent, and to the heirs, Exec's, & assignee or assignees of the other eight patentees, and to their respective heirs and assigns forever; and the said tract of land so patented as aforesaid, and all that our and every of our right & claim to the interest or demand whatsoever of, in, or to the said tract of land & every part & parcel thereof, TO HAVE AND TO HOLD the same tract of land and premises unto the said David Jamison, and the heirs, Exec's, assignee or assignees of the other patentees aforesaid, and to their respective heirs & assigns forever. IN WITNESS whereof we have hereunto put our hands and seals this Thirteenth day of October, in the year 1730.

Perpuwas	his mark
Sasaragua	her mark
Makerin	his mark
Memram	his mark
Shawanachko	his mark
Shawasquo	his mark
Tounis, Son of Shawasquo	his m.
Acgans	his mark
Nimham	his mark
Ouracgacguis	his mark
Taguahams	his mark
Seeck	his mark
Cocewyn	his mark
Mamany	his mark

Meeorandum—that the words "John Aertson," between lines 8 & 9 from the bottom, & the words "do by these presents give, grant, bargain, sell, release and confirm," between lines 6 & 7 from the bottom, were enterlined before sealing and delivery.

A rye, Seeck's Son	his mark
Wappenas	his mark
Tintgeme	her mark

30

Ayawatask	his mark
Nonnaparee	his mark
Kindtquaw	his mark

SEALED AND DELIVERED by Shawanachko and Shawasco, and Tounis his Son, in the presence of us.

Phillip Cortlandt,
John Crooke, Junior,
Robert Benson,
Lymon Arygier.

Sealed and delivered in the presence of us.

Barant Vankleeck,
Tealk Tietsoort,
Frans La Roy,
Joseph Webb,
Henry Vanderburgh,
Jacobus V. D. Boogert,
The mark of H. O. Hendrick Ostrom,
The mark of X Jonas Scott.

On the back of the deed appears the following endorsements, showing that a not very high consideration was demanded for the property.

ENDORSEMENTS

Received the thirteenth day of October, in the year of our Lord one thousand seven hundred and thirty, of and by the hands of Mr. Henry Filkins, for all the land in full formerly granted by Patent and now sold by an Indian Deed for and in consideration of certain sums of money, goods and merchandise, to the value of one hundred and fifty pounds, to us Acgans & Nimham, Principal Sachemache and Proprietors, in behalf of all the rest, in hand paid by Mr. Henry Filkins as aforesaid, for the use of Mr. David Jamison, the only surviving patentee of said patent and Indian Deed, and to the heirs Exec's, and assignee or assignees of the other eight patentees, and to their respective heirs and assigns forever, the said sum of one hundred and fifty pounds, being in full for the said tract of Land according to the Limitts and Bounds within mentioned as wittness our hands and seals the day and year above mentioned, only excepting still the Whrits of some North Indians that are . . . . which we since except.

The mark af Acgans,
Nimham, his mark.

Signed and sealed in the presence of us.

Henry Van Derburgh,
Barant Van Kleeck,
Frans La Roy,
Jacobes V. D. Boogert.

BE IT REMEMBERED, that on the fourth day of November, in the year of our Lord one thousand seven hundred and thirty-seven, personally came and appeared before me, Philip Courtlandt, one of his Majesty's Councill for the Province of New York, Shawanachko and Shawasquo, two of the Indians within named, and acknowledged the within Deed to be their and each of their Voluntary Act and Deed, and that they executed the same for the uses therein mentioned; and also confessed and declared that they had respectively received the goods following, to witt, the said Shawanachko three striped Blanketts, three Dufills Blanketts, four Dozen of pipes, ten knives, two Hatchets, one Strouds Blankett, six pounds of powder, ten pounds of lead, two white shirts, and One Gunn.

And the said Shawasquo seven striped Blanketts, seven Duffills Blankets, eight Dozen of pipes, twenty knives, five hatchets, one Strouds Blankett, eighteen pounds of powder, eighteen pounds of Lead, and one good gun, four white shirts, and one half barrel of strong beer, in full satisfaction of and for of consideration of their Respective shares, right and title of, in, and to the within Tract of Land—the words, "two white shirts" and "four white shirts" being interlined.

Phillip Cortlandt.

This map of Dutchess County shows the relation of Pleasant Valley to the Great Nine Partners Patent, and the relation of Dutchess County to the State of New York.

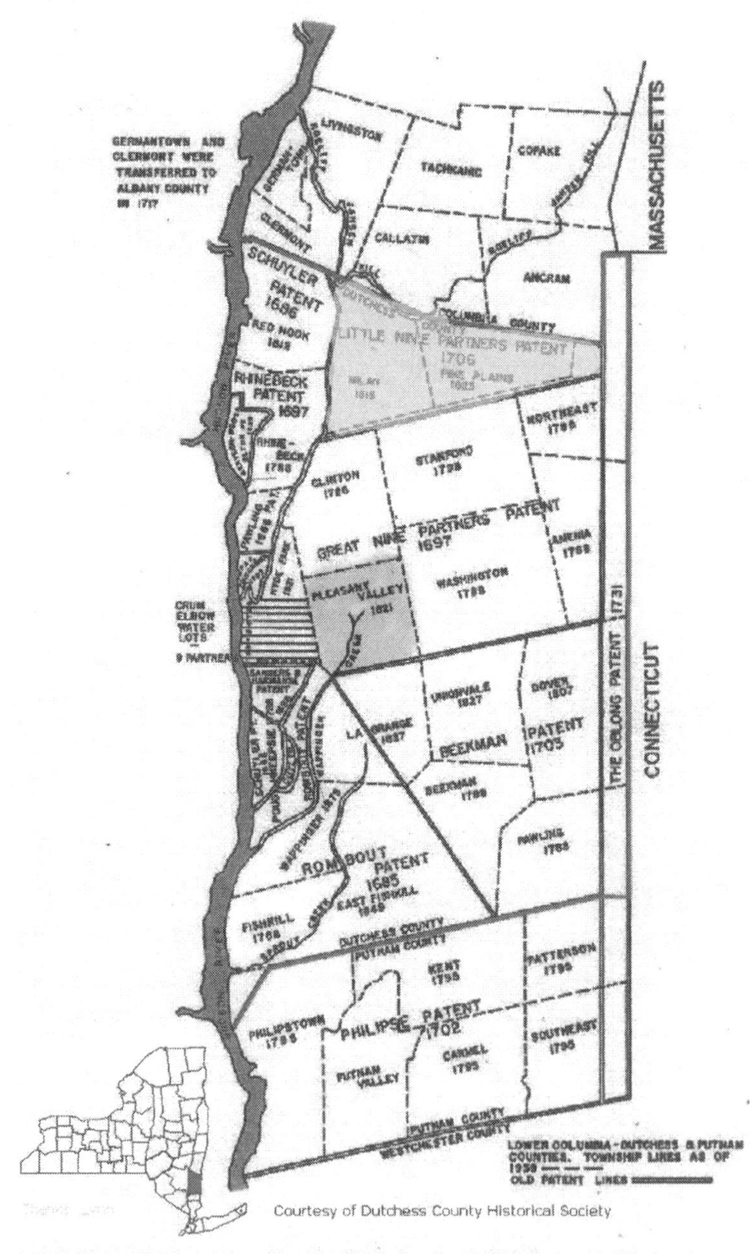

http://www.rootsweb.ancestry.com/~nylnphs/Images/L9P_MAP.JPG (Date 6/7/2012)

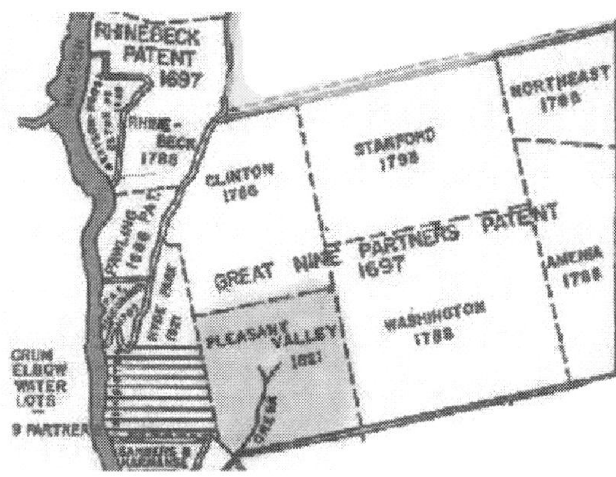

The lower left portion of the Great Nine Partners Patent would later become Pleasant Valley.

Although the date of the Patent was 1697, the land wasn't opened for settlement until the 1730's. For some prospective settlers leasing land was their only option because they didn't have the money to buy land.[b] The heirs of the original patent owners opened tracts of land for settlement[c]

Charlotte Precinct was settled about 1750, it comprised Stanford, Clinton, and Washington. March 7, 1788 an act was passed dividing New York State into fourteen counties, which were divided into townships instead of precincts. [d]

On January 26, 1821, a bill was passed by the State Legislature creating the towns of Hyde Park and Pleasant Valley from the town of Clinton, which after defining the boundaries of the former town, reads:

> "And be it further enacted that the remaining part of the said town of Clinton shall be divided into two separate towns by the following division line to, wit:
>
> Beginning on the west line of the town of Washington in the corner made by lots number five and six in the great division of the Nine Partners Patent and running westerly along said lot line until it intersects the east line of the aforesaid town of Hyde Park, and that the north of the two last mentioned towns shall be known by the name of Clinton, * * * and that the south of the last mentioned towns shall be known by the name of Pleasant Valley, and that the first town meeting in said town last mentioned shall be held at the house of Cyrus Berry, on the first Tuesday of April next."[e]

At that time the population of Pleasant Valley was about 700, it was the commercial center of town, with Salt Point and Washington Hollow as hamlets. Because the Wappingers Creek flowed through the town many mills were built along the creek. Pleasant Valley became a manufacturing center, as the population grew the residents petitioned the government for a post office, in 1813, it was granted. Another petition went to the Legislature for an act of incorporation. By that act the following village trustees were appointed: John Robert Abbott, John Beadle, Israel Dean, Hubby Adee and Joshua Ward, to serve until the second Tuesday of May, 1815. There are no records of elections until May 9, 1843, when William Thorne, Franklin Dudley, Zachariah S. Flagler, Gilbert Noxon and Joel Terrill were elected trustees.[f]

Over the years many cotton and grain mills and farms brought growth to Pleasant Valley, it became a prosperous town. During the late 1800's and early 1900's two railroads ran through the town, carrying goods and summer visitors, the town had three hotels in the center of town, and many large homes in the countryside became boarding houses. The Main Street was picturesque, lined with trees, homes had picket fences in front.

As early as the 1700's there was a mill on the site just west of the bridge over the Wappingers Creek. The February 17, 1796 issue of the Poughkeepsie Journal contained he following advertising:

> "For Sale
>
> The Farm and Mills at Pleasant Valley, situate eight miles east of Poughkeepsie on the main Nine-Partner road to Sharon, Dover, &c.
>
> The farm consists 110 acres of land, and about 25 acres woodland. 30 acres the best meadow, a good orchard and large garden with a variety of fruit trees, asparagus bed, &c., a good dwelling house, and well of water near the kitchen, a large new Dutch Barn, barracks &c., with convenient outhouses.
>
> The mill stands on the Wappingers Creek (a never failing stream of water), is large and strong, three stories high, 75 feet long by thirty feet wide, calculated for the Flouring business on a large scale, two run of stones, the one burr and the other Esopus; the bolts and other works made on the best and easiest construction for expediting work; a great share of country work, &c., the place well situated for the purchased of grain, a fine wheat country, a public road.
>
> On the premises is a good stone house and potash works;

adjoining the mill is a large and commodious store for dry goods and groceries, at which place business has been done for many years.

Should it better suit the purchaser the on-half and undivided moiety of the above estate will be sold; the mill separate from the farm; the whole together.

In case the above are not sold by 11th of April next will on that day be sold at public auction at the Tontine Coffee-House in New York.

Jacob K. Duryea	
John M. Thursten	Executors of the estate of
John Duryea, Jun.	John Duryea
Jacob Smith	dec'd

December 10th, 1795"[g]

In 1979, Gail Crotty, then Pleasant Valleys town Historian did a through report on activities of the mill as they were in 1870. ...she found that of the 432 families then residents of Pleasant Valley, 41 lived off of the cotton mill in the center of town...She also discovered that of the nearly 80 people employed at the mill during the Garner years, one third of them were under the age of 16, and some were as young as 8 years old.[h]

Over the years the mill has been a important part of the town history. First a bell, then a whistle to alert the volunteer fireman of a fire was located on the mill. Someone at the mill answered the phone when a call came to report a fire, many of the mill workers were fireman and were allowed to drop what they were doing to answer the call for help.

The site where the mill once stood is now the Mill Site Memorial Park, which includes Memorial Stones, Eternal Flame and Veteran's Bricks on the creek side, with lawn, gardens, paths in the depressed footprint of the old mill and the mill stone in the center. There is also a gazebo with sidewalks. The original mill store still stands and houses the Town Historical Museum.

This picture is the way the mill would have looked in 1911.(GBG)

The mill as it was in 1922.(GBG)

The back side of the mill, circa 1911.

During the early 1930's the mill was incorporated as the "Pleasant Valley Finishing Company" that's when the 140 foot tall water tower was added.[i]
circa 1980
(Even though the name was legally changed,
most locals still refer to it as "The Mill.")

During that time fabric was dyed at the mill, there were times when the creek would turn colors below the mill. After sometime vats were built to pump the dye into so it could separate from the water, and the water could be released into the creek and the dye was taken to various dump sites. There were still times when the creek could be seen colored. During the 1960's and early 1970's material from the mill was sold in a store across the street in the cement block building that had been the first fire house. The Pleasant Valley Finishing Company continued operations until about 1980 when they slowly started moving operations to the Schats-Federal Bearing factory on Fairview Avenue in Poughkeepie. By the end of August 1984 the factory was empty. [j]

The deserted factory. (GBG)

The building stayed empty, the water tower was a place for energetic youngsters to climb and write their names, the factory windows were broken, ivy seemed to be taking over the building as it was deteriorating.

On Thursday, July 21, 1994 smoke was seen coming out of the roof, the fire department was called, soon flames broke through the roof.

Volunteer firemen fighting the blaze as the mill burns.

The bell tower can be seen through the smoke.

The mill as the fire is almost out and the building is almost gone.

An aerial view of the mill after the fire. In this picture the water tower is still standing. The area where it was is now, the Pleasant Valley Mill Site Park and Museum and McDonalds.

Aftermath of the fire. circa 1994 (GBG)

The water tower falling down as the burned building mill site was cleaned up. circa 1995

The empty shell of the mill as seen from South Avenue, across the Wappingers Creek. circa 1995 (PH)

The Mill Site Historical Building, the only building that remains. (TeddiS)

From around 1905 until 1965 the Democratic Party ruled Pleasant Valley. One of the ways the candidates campaigned, was to give out candy bars, cigars and these desk blotters.

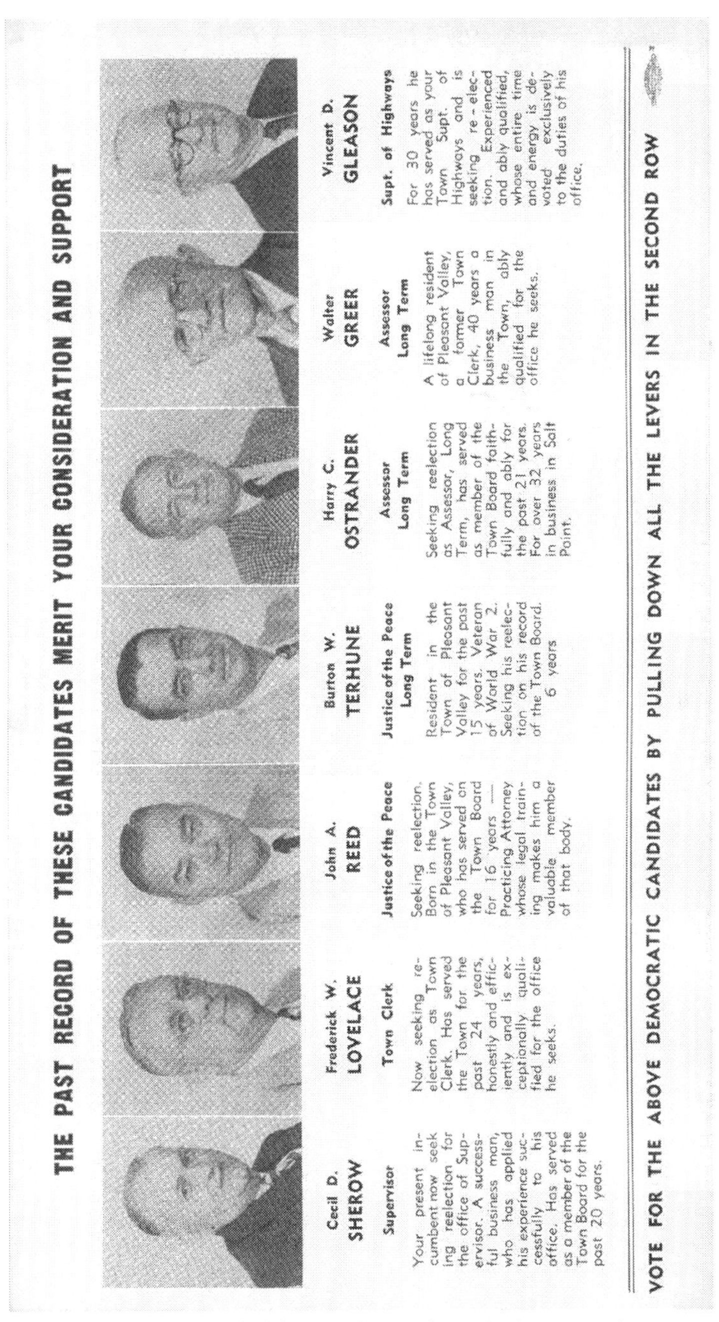

This is the desk blotter from the 1953 campaign.

In 1965 a headline in the November 3, 1965 Poughkeepsie Journal, page was "**Dairyman Wigsten Elected First Republican Supervisor In 60 Years in Pleasant Valley.**" Warren Wigsten was elected the first Republican Supervisor of Pleasant Valley to follow the Democratic rule of Cecil Sherow. In order to list the Supervisors I had help from Gary Veeder, Penny Hickman and Warren Wigsten. We have put together the following list:

Cecil Sherow, Warren Wigsten, Mike Cady, John Stewart, James Geary, Gary Veeder, Dave Gardner, Cliff Andrews, Tom Hankamp, Penny Hickman (first woman, served for 12 years), John McNair, Jeff Battistoni, Frank Suscynski, John McNair (his second not consecutive term) Carl Tomik, current Supervisor.[k]

During the 1950's when IBM came to Poughkeepsie, then expanded into East Fishkill, houses were built to accommodate the growing number of families who moved into the area. The "down-sizing" of IBM in the early 1990's did not seem to slow the population growth of Pleasant Valley, many residents still commute from Pleasant Valley to their jobs.

The face of Pleasant Valley has changed, there are no more mills, or hotels, Main Street is paved, the large trees are gone, replaced by flower beds, or small trees. There are sidewalks along Main Street, with crosswalks at the intersections, and signal lights.

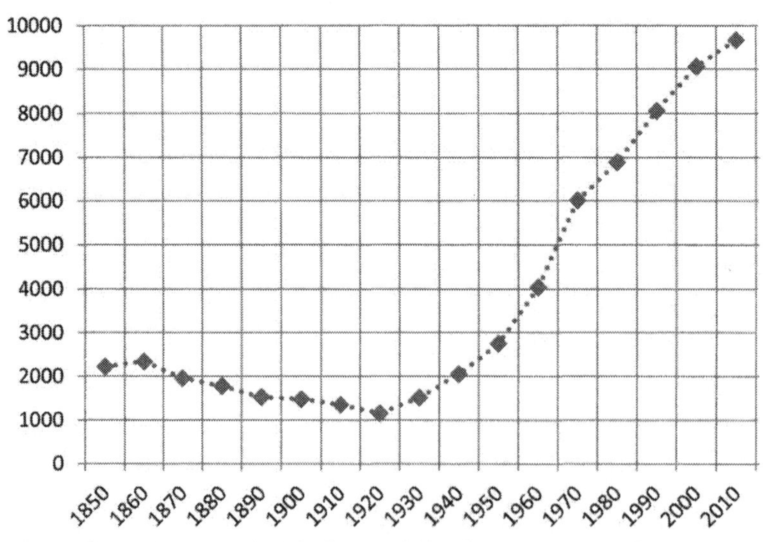

The census numbers are from the government website (http://2010.census.gov/2010census/popmap/ipmtext.php)

An aerial view of Pleasant Valley during the Sesquicentennial Parade of 1971. This is looking down on the Presbyterian Church and cemetery, the town hall and ball field.

An aerial view of Pleasant Valley during the Sesquicentennial Parade of 1971. This is the center of town looking west along Main Street, the construction on the left is what became the Grand Union then Key Foods and is now Dollar General.

Street Scenes - Early Days

During the late 1800's and early 1900's Pleasant Valley was a tourist destination for people from as far away as New York City. Families might come up to Poughkeepsie on the train from New York City, or the Hudson River Day Liner, and then take the train to Pleasant Valley.

Picture from Life Magazine online.

The Hudson River Day Liner as it might have looked as it left the Poughkeepsie dock.

The Pleasant Valley Railroad station, from a postcard.

There were several Hotels in the center of the village, and some families took in summer boarders.

The tree lined streets were bustling; local hotels and store keepers were prosperous. It may be hard for us now to think of Pleasant Valley as a resort town, but as you look at the pictures on the following pages, you can imagine what a nice place it was to rest from the hustle and bustle of city life.

Garage and gas station, along Route 44 as you entered the town.

This gas station was at the corner of Niagara Road and Route 44, later it was a foreign car repair shop, run by John Briggs. In 1966 it was a TV repair and sales store, on the end facing the village, run by Ken and Millie Hinsch. The other end housed a bakery. It has been a bicycle shop since 1973.

This picture was taken by the electric company when they erected the utility pole along Main Street in front of the Pleasant Valley Ford Garage. The date is unknown, but it would have been in the early 1900's.

These pictures were taken throughout the town as utility poles were placed. This is currently the site of the CVS store and parking lot at the corner of Main Street and West Road.

Main Street: The first white building on the left is now gone, the next building is now the Department Store. (FS)

The picture for this postcard was taken from just a little left and farther back of the previous one.

Looking down North Avenue from Main Street, these homes and trees no longer exist. (FS)

Hadden's Store: on the Northeast corner of Main Street and North Avenue. It is now a gas station and garage. Circa 1915

Main Street: looking east from intersection of North Avenue would be Hadden's store on the left. It is currently a gas station and a garage. Circa 1915(FS)

This view is what would be seen, if you were looking east on Main Street. The building second from the right was the Pleasant Valley Hotel, and the street to the left is North Avenue. (FS)

This Postcard was published by G. E. Lovelace, who owned a store on Main Street. This view is Main Street, looking west from North Avenue circa,1930. (FS)

Main Street, looking east from North Avenue. The building on the right in later years was Pleasant Valley Hotel, next would be Devine's store. Both are now gone to make way for strip mall.(FS)

A barber shop, unknown location.

Main Street with picket fence: it was needed to keep farm animals out of yards as they were driven down the street.

Main Street looking east: on left is the Methodist church and John Knott house which was replaced by stores and Charcoal Pit restaurant in 1955. It is now the Fire Department driveway and NAPA Store.

Main Street looking east toward the covered bridge: The Mill and Dr. LeRoy's office was on the right. Dr. LeRoy's office is now McDonalds. Circa 1908 (FS)

Dr. LeRoy's home, on Main Street, razed in 1953 to enlarge the Pleasant Valley Finishing Company.

2011 Lovelace's Hall, Pleasant Valley N. Y.

Originally the building in the center was known as Lovelace Hall. During the 1930's the interior was divided into two sections, a porch and stairs were added, from the mid-1930's to 1950 the left side housed the Post Office. Later it was the dentist's office of Dr. Nosonowitz. In 1982 the left side opened as the "Past 'n' Perfect", a ladies consignment boutique, with new, nearly new or aged to perfection clothes, furs, jewelry & accessories.

At some point the doors that had been in the center were moved to the outer sides so that the right side door would be farther away from the Methodist Church. The right side became a liquor store, and that side is now a frame shop.

The small building on the left had been a tack shop on South Avenue before it was moved to its current location in 1915. At this location it became a barber shop, first operated by Hank Kesler, then from sometime in the 1940's Bob Turcott ran the barbershop. Carl Rennia has been the barber since 1971 and continues the tradition to this day.

The building on the right with the flag is the G.E. Lovelace Store. Over the years it has been an ice cream store, a meat market and a restaurant, it is currently vacant. In front of the car there is a town well.(FS)

The man in the center with the white shirt and suspenders is George E. Lovelace, the store owner, and in front of him are his daughter and son.

This picture is of the inside of the G. E. Lovelace Store.

During 1910 Mr. Lovelace sold these calendar plates.
The feathers on the headdress are months.

The covered bridge over the Wappingers Creek. The fence connects to the bridge to keep the sheep from wandering off the edge and ending up in the Wappingers Creek. The sign on the bridge warns people in cars to drive at only 4 miles per hour. Circa 1908 (FS)

Main Street: covered bridge, Kay's house and carriage shop are on the left, mill in background, Circa 1908.

Donaldson- VanReusen, site of blacksmith shop for over 100 years.

L. H. Wilbur Blacksmith Shop across from the Presbyterian Church. (MB)

L. H. Wilbur Blacksmith Shop Circa 1906

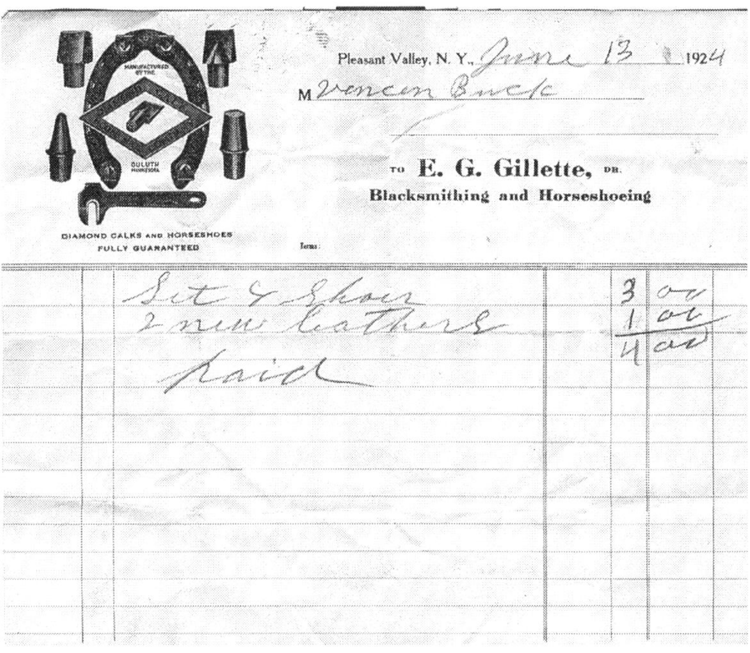

MANUFACTURED BY THE
DULUTH MINNESOTA
DIAMOND CALKS AND HORSESHOES
FULLY GUARANTEED

Pleasant Valley, N. Y., June 13 1924

M Vernon Buck

To E. G. Gillette, Dr.

Blacksmithing and Horseshoeing

Terms:

Set 4 Shoes	3	00
2 new leathers	1	00
	4	00
Paid		

There was no picture of the G. E. Gillette Blacksmithing and Horseshoeing shop, the building was on South Avenue on the right side about a quarter mile down.

These horses are being led from the driveway across from South Avenue. The building on the left was Wolvais Meat Market and later the home of Fred Lovelace and his family for many years. Fred was the Pleasant Valley Town Clerk and Tax Collector for over 25 years starting in 1928.

Looking across Main Street toward South Avenue. The Library was on the left. Notice the clothes on a clothes line on right middle of picture. The only house still standing at present is the one on the right side of South Avenue with the little porch.

Martin & Virginia Berry's house was the first house on left on South Avenue. It was torn down to make a parking lot for a telephone company substation.

Looking at South Avenue from across Main Street. The two story house on the right later became the Soldier's Memorial in 1949. It was moved to the Mill Site Historical Park 2004. I lived in the small white house, with the little front porch for 25 years, from 1979 to 2004. The steps, on the left and the house on the left are gone, replaced by a telephone company substation and parking lot. In the center of the picture, down the street there is a large white building which had been a boarding house in the early days of the mill. It was a four family home that burned in 1953. (FS)

This postcard is of the dam over the Wappingers Creek sometime before 1957. After 1957 the dam was lowered due to flooding in the town.

Post card of house on the edge of the Wappingers Creek, near the bridge.
This house is partly visible in the previous picture of the dam and bridge.

View from Miles Carroll's hill on South Avenue of the Pleasant Valley Finishing Company, covered bridge and Wappingers Creek. Circa 1880 (GBG)

William "Bucky" Storms with the Wolvais Meat wagon.

The Wappingers Creek was a place for fishing and picnicking for residents and vacationers. This picture is of the creek, above the dam.

About a quarter mile up Creek Road, there was a path leading down to the Wappingers Creek, to a very popular swimming area. During the 1950's there were two areas next to each other. They were referred to as "Steep Rock" and "Sandy Bottom." At "Steep Rock" we jumped in from the rock, and at "Sandy Bottom" the water is more shallow, where you could walk into the water.

Picture taken from the top of the hill as you entered the village, the house on the right is the former Albert Husted home, and was a Quaker boarding school. from 1809 to 1819.

Bowman's Grist Mill, built in 1808, burned down in 1915 and was rebuilt. Was Daniel Dean's calico mill in 1810, later it was owned by John Belding. The mill is across from Albrecht's farm on Route 44, near St. Paul's Church.

Kenyon Mill, then Bower's (1850's to 80's) This mill no longer exists.

This house belonged to a family named Velie, it is about two miles up Traver Road and is now the home of the Rawls family at Bilmar Nursery. It was the site of Ward's mill.

Street Scenes - Mid-20th Century

During the 1940's many changes came to Pleasant Valley the following pictures depict a much different town from what it was like near the turn of the century.

During the 1950's Mr. Sutherland often went shopping in the village with his horse and sulky. In this picture he is passing the G. E. Masten Feed Store. (PC/TeddiS)

G. E. Masten Feed Store as it was before the 1968 fire.

When you shopped at the feed store you would be waited on by either Donald or Wesley Drake. The two bachelors lived next door to the store.

This is Donald probably working on the books for the store.

This is the home where Donald and Wesley Drake lived. It is on West Road just past the Feed Store. circa 2012 (RV)

Looking east on route 44 from near West Road, Pleasant Valley Ford Garage on the left, it is now CVS pharmacy.

This building was across the street from the Presbyterian Church. Over the years this was many different kinds of stores, a grocery store, comic book store, it was torn down to make way for the entrance to the CVS store.

Map of the town during 1967.

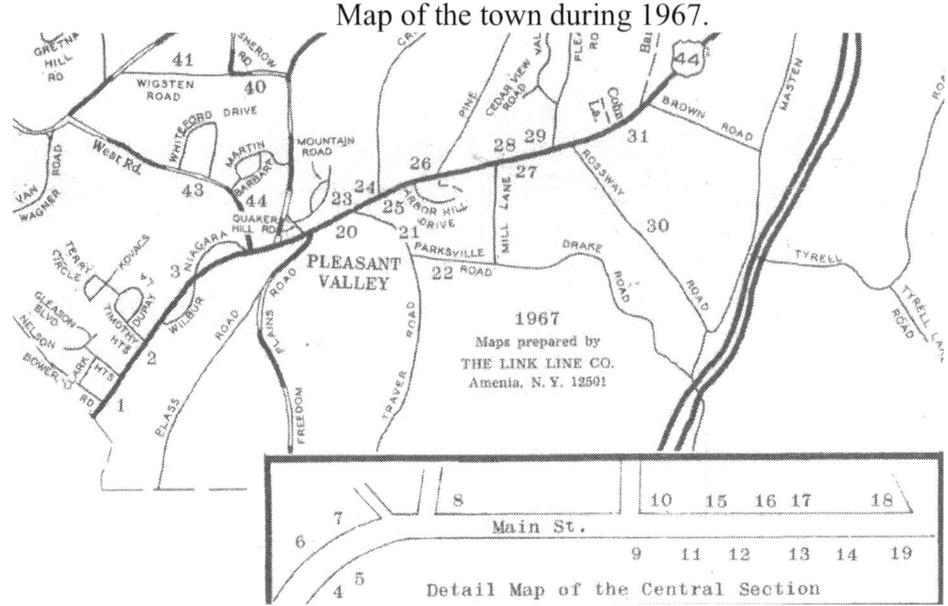

Key to stores:

- 1 Rudy's Market
- 2 Antique Arms
- 3 Freisitzer Elec. Cont.
- 4 Bill's Sinclair Station
- 5 Bower Memorials
- 6 Pastryland Bakery
- 7 Ken's TV Sales & Serv.
- 8 Pleasant Valley Garage
- 9 Pleasant Valley Hotel "Cady's"
- 10 Van's Service Station
- 11 Valley Market
- 12 Costello's Rest.
- 13 Elmer Nygren, Inc
- 14 George T.Whalen, Inc
- 15 Allen Funeral Home
- 16 Valley Vogues, Inc
- 17 Marine Midland Bank
- 18 Pleasant Valley Grill "Chick's"
- 19 Pleasant Valley Finishing Co.
- 20 Valley Motel & Colonial House Rest.
- 21 Armstrong & Moran Ref.
- 22 Albrecht's Dairy
- 24 j & H Russell Co.
- 25 De Groodt Bros.
- 26 Conklin Inst. Corp.
- 27 Clayton Haight's Garage
- 28 Hankamp Auto
- 29 Kiwi Riding Supplies
- 30 Gordon Daley Lawn Service
- 31 Kirchhoff Bros. Liquor Store
- 43 Homer Teal & sons
- 44 Pleasant Valley Plumbing & Heating

South side of Main Street, these buildings are gone, and have been replaced by a strip mall, with The Country Thistle, Marion's Spa, a travel agency and a bank. circa 1968

Another view of Main Street, circa 1968.

Main Street, looking east from the center of the village: the first building on the right is currently the post office, next is a restaurant, McDonald's and the Mill Site historic building.

Main Street, looking across the bridge, sometime before 2000.

Main Street as you enter the village from the east, The Roadhouse, Frame Shop & Past and Perfect, barber shop, storage building for NAPA store, and NAPA store.

This house is at the corner of Stream Lane and Quaker Hill Road, it was the home of the Brinckerhoff family. Photo circa 1947 (GBG)

On Route 44 across from Timothy Heights, was a bar called "Mickey's" during the late 1940's or 1950's. It was also a furniture repair store, during 1967 it was Antique Arms, now it is "The Barn" which sells used clothes and furniture.

Along the south side of Route 44, a little west of Timothy Heights, was Karl Steffen's bar, later "Club 44" while still a bar it had many different names. It was also a lumber/hardware store, a video shop, it is currently a chiropractor office.

This was the "Stone Chimney" it was along Route 44 at the east end of Wilbur Road.

Palmers was along Route 44, east of Pleasant Valley. Joan and Al Palmer owned and operated it for many years, after the death of her husband, Joan continued to operate this and apartments that were built alongside it until the late 1970's when she retired.

This building has housed many different restaurants, it is currently vacant.

Roads and Bridges

In the early days the products of various mills were carted over the narrow, rutted and muddy Filkintown Road, southwest to Poughkeepsie and east to the New England states. It is believed that the original road ran between the creek and the present Main Street, behind the present Presbyterian Church and the old houses on that side of the street. This is the belief because three of the oldest houses were apparently built to face the creek instead of Main Street.

According to Mrs. F. Irving (Irene) Bower, lifelong resident and local historian, The Filkintown road was taken over by the Dutchess Turnpike Company and became a toll road in 1806. Two six-cent tolls were collected in Pleasant Valley, one in front of the Andrew Skidmore house east of the village, near Mill Lane, and the other where Bower Road begins just west of the village.

An article in the Poughkeepsie paper dated December 24th, 1810 stated: "The Turnpike Gate No. 1 may be moved from time to time to any place northerly of its present situation, not exceeding two miles, to catch people avoiding the toll by going around the toll gate."

The company that collected the tolls folded after the blizzard of 1888 because it couldn't afford to clear the road.

The first local bridge is said to have been built about 1745 or 1750 as a part of the old Filkintown road across the creek near Fitzpatrick's hotel. This was more in the center of the hamlet, near what is currently the location Maggiacomo Lane. It would have been accessed by going down South Avenue or the road to Oswego, as it was called at that time, about a quarter mile.

The route of the road was changed, and another bridge was put across the creek where the bridge stands today. This early bridge was carried away in the flood of 1848, and replaced by the covered bridge that was used until 1911. The old covered bridge had, in its last years, a sign at either end with this warning, "Automobiles slow down To 4 Miles an Hour". And so the "Horse and Buggy Days" were coming to an end in Pleasant Valley.

According to Mrs. Bower droves of cattle used to go up and down the road. Chester Husted told of a time that a paling on the bridge was loose when a herd of sheep was going across. One sheep went into the creek, all the other sheep followed and were drowned. [1]

The September 18, 1911 issue of the Poughkeepsie Eagle contains an article headlined:

"Town of Pleasant Valley Brings Action in the Supreme Court to Legalize Issue to Cover Cost of New Bridge." Article further states: "The Town of Pleasant Valley brought action in the Supreme Court here Saturday to legalize its recent bond issue to cover the cost of the new concrete bridge at Pleasant Valley. The action will go on record of being the first of its kind in this county and it is probably the first case of the kind in the state. The bonds recently issued were bought by I. W. Sherrill, of this city, who afterword found that they were irregular in some technical respect and in order to prevent the bonds being invalidated the action was taken.

On the application of Supervisor Charles L. Cole, through his attorney Clarence Drake, to Judge Morschauser, the court Saturday signed an order finding that the issue of bonds substantially comply with the statute." So the new concrete bridge could be built.

An article in the May 7, 1911 Sunday Courier, a predecessor of the Poughkeepsie Journal lamented the passing of the area's few remaining covered bridges: "The old covered bridge over the Wappingers Creek at Pleasant Valley has been torn down to make way for a modern steel and concrete bridge which will be erected this season to replace it"

A new cement arch bridge was built in 1911 to replace the covered bridge. That bridge remained until 1941, when it was replaced with a bridge that had six foot high steel girders. In 2000 the road was widened, turn lanes were added, and sidewalks were added or widened along the highway on the east side of the bridge.

The covered bridge as it looked as you were entering town from the east in 1908.

View of the covered bridge in the early 1900's, Kay's carriage shop in the center.

Covered bridge with the mill on the left.

The covered bridge postcard taken about 1806.

Arched bridge that replaced the covered bridge in 1911.

The large building in the center of the picture is the boarding house that was used for mill workers.

The arched bridge, taken when the creek was so low that no water is going over the dam. Date unknown but it is thought to be 1912.

The Arch Bridge over Wappinger's Creek, Pleasant Valley, N. Y.

Postcard published courtesy of Dieter Friedrichsen.

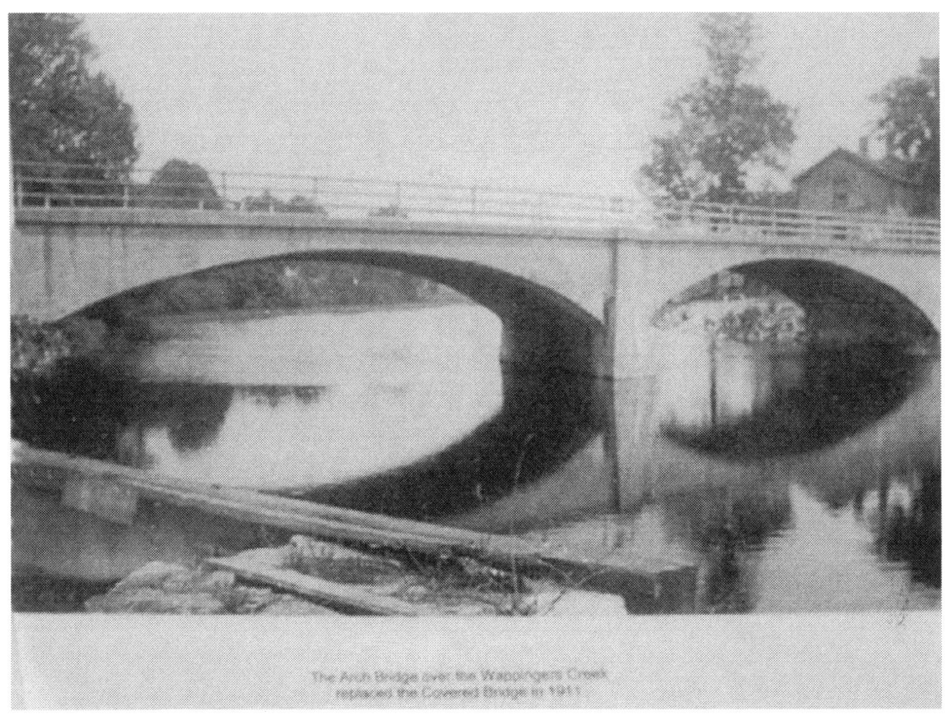

The Arch Bridge over the Wappingers Creek
replaced the Covered Bridge in 1911

The bridge with steel girders that was built in 1941 to replace the arched bridge.

This picture of the steel girder bridge was taken in 1999 when the state was getting ready to remove it and replace it with a wider bridge with turning lane.

View from the current bridge looking toward the village, circa 2010 (TeddiS)

As you traveled the roads outside the village of Pleasant Valley between 1930 and 1940 these are some of the roads you may have seen.

According to notes by Martin Berry this might be the bridge east of St. Paul's Episcopal Church on Route 44.

Edward Roosevelt DeGroff Bridge
Junction of Sherow Road and North Avenue taken 1931

Edward Roosevelt DeGroff home taken late 1931
Junction of Sherow Road and North Avenue.

Listed as Allison Laird Bridge 1929 in the George Greenwood file circa 1929

Doty's bridge, circa 1939

Hibernia Road Bridge, west of Junction with Scout Road, circa 1936, this bridge was washed away in the flood of 1955 and replaced by a bridge with a steel bed.

Salt Point Bridge looking downstream from pond circa 1936

Railroad

The station for the P&E (Poughkeepsie & Eastern) railroad was located behind The Armstrong Hotel. It was in operation from May 1, 1871, until July 1937. The tracks came over the hill where Niagara Road is and crossed West Road where Station Road is now, next to CVS.

Lady's waiting for the train.

RAILROAD STATION, PLEASANT VALLEY, N. Y.
PHOT. & PUB. BY L. S. HORTON, HYDE PARK, N. Y.

Post card from (FS)

After the trains stopped running in 1937, the original Pleasant Valley railroad station was used as a home to several different families and as storage for the Ford Garage, Pleasant Valley's first car dealership.

One of the families who lived there in the 1940's while Mr. and Mrs. Miles Carroll owned the building was the Silvernail family. When Bill Silvernail was asked if the home had running water, he replied' "We had running water, you had to run and get it."

The station as it looked when it was rented as a home.

The Railroad Station as it looked when it was restored in the 1970's and moved to the D'Aquannis Intermediate School on West Road. (TS)

According to the town historian Olive Doty, in 1912 ten trains a day stopped in Pleasant Valley. There were 422 passengers on the 3:25 PM train to Poughkeepsie that Labor Day. During those times Pleasant Valley was a resort town and get away for people from New York City, Poughkeepsie or other large cities. There were several hotels and boarding houses. Swimming, boating and fishing were available in the Wappingers Creek. The train was a much more convenient form of transportation than horse and wagon. A person could ride the train or boat up the Hudson from New York City area and then get the train in Poughkeepsie to Pleasant Valley for a reasonable rate.

Postcard of train tracks leaving Pleasant Valley; this is where Niagara Road is now. The road in the picture is Route 44; the house that you can see over the billboard was the residence of Herb Wilbur and family.

Below are examples of train passes that were used by the Doty family.

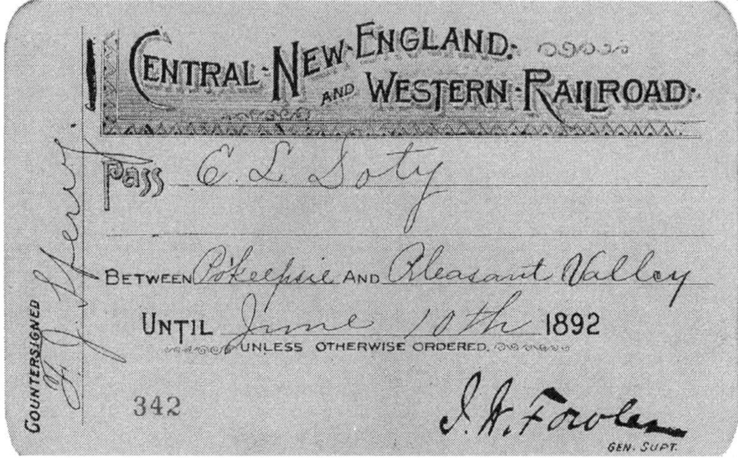

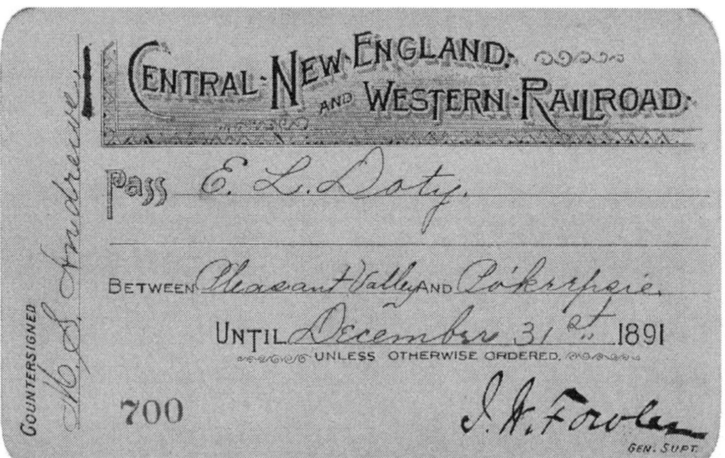

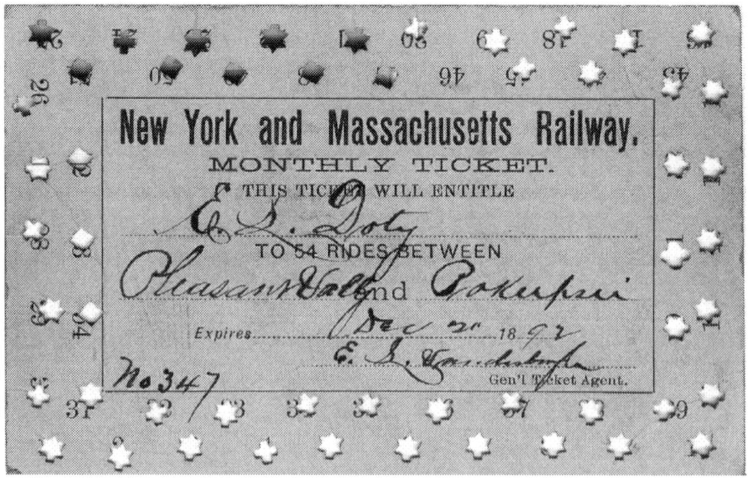

Schedule of Fares.

From Poughkeepsie.	Single Fare.	Excursion.	Between New York and Stations on the P. & E. R'y. via N. Y. C. & H. R. R. R. Single Fare.	Excursion.	via Hudson River Day Line. Single Fare.	Excursion.
Van Wagner's	.15	.25	....	....	....	....
Pleasant Valley	.20	.35	1.86	3.70	1.35	2.10
Salt Point	.30	.50	1.96	3.75	1.40	2.30
Clinton Corners	.35	.60	2.01	3.75	1.41	2.30
Upton Lake Park	....	*.25	....	*2.00	....	....
Willow Brook	.45	.80	....	3.75	....	....
Stanfordville	.50	.85	2.10	3.85	1.55	2.60
McIntyre	.57	.95	....	3.75	....	....
Stissing	.60	1.00	2.10	3.75	1.70	2.95
Pine Plains	.75	1.15	2.21	3.60	1.80	3.10
Ancram Lead Mines.	.90	1.55	....	....	1.90	3.50
Halstead's	.95	....	....	....	....	....
Tanner's	1.00	....	....	....	....	....
Boston Corners	1.10	1.90	....	....	2.16	3.80

* These Special Excursion Rate Tickets to Upton Lake Park are good only on the day sold, and between the points named on the tickets and in the direction indicated thereon.

...THE...
Poughkeepsie
...AND...
Eastern
Railway
TIME TABLE
...AND...
CONNECTIONS
IN EFFECT
Sunday, May 30, 1897.

POUGHKEEPSIE, HARTFORD & BOSTON RAIL ROAD
OCT. 11, 1878

READ DOWN 2 [illegible] AM	4 [illegible] PM	8 [illegible] AM		READ UP 5 [illegible] PM	3 [illegible] PM	1 [illegible] AM
11:00	5:25	9:30	POUGHKEEPSIE	5:30	5:20	8:43
11:11	5:34	9:41	VAN WAGNER'S	5:20	5:08	8:33
11:21	5:42	9:48	PLEASANT VALLEY	5:12	4:59	8:25
*11:28	*5:49	*9:55	RUSSEL'S	*5:05	*4:48	*8:18
11:40	5:56	10:04	SALT POINT	4:57	4:40	8:10
11:52	6:03	10:13	CLINTON CORNERS	4:49	4:26	8:02
12:04	6:11	10:22	WILLOW BROOK	4:41	4:12	7:54
12:18	6:20	10:30	STANFORDVILLE	4:34	3:53	7:47
12:27	6:26	10:37	M^c INTYRE	4:27	3:42	7:40
12:34	6:30	10:42	STISSING	4:23	3:34	7:36
12:56	6:55	2:16	PINE PLAINS	4:20	3:10	7:20
1:07	7:10	2:32	ANCRAM LEAD MINES	3:40	2:53	7:03

The trains were used not only for passengers and coal, but for hauling ice, milk from the farms and cloth from the mills south to New York City and east to New England.

Workers gathering ice to be shipped on the P&E Railroad. (GBG)

P&E Engine 10 with the crew.

By 1938 the last of the east-west rails from Columbia County south to Poughkeepsie and Hopewell Junction in Dutchess County were torn out. The rails were sold for scrap to Japan.

The P&E Railroad had been in operation about 16 years before the big railroad bridge in Poughkeepsie was completed in 1888. The bridge company had intentions of acquiring the P&E Railroad to connect eastward across Dutchess County to reach railroads in Connecticut. The management of P&E would not sell the railroad to the bridge company. To get around this problem, the bridge company built a 28 mile long railroad parallel to the P&E and called it the P&C (Poughkeepsie & Connecticut).

There were places along the line where the two competing railroads were only a few feet apart. Near Salt Point they crossed in an open field.

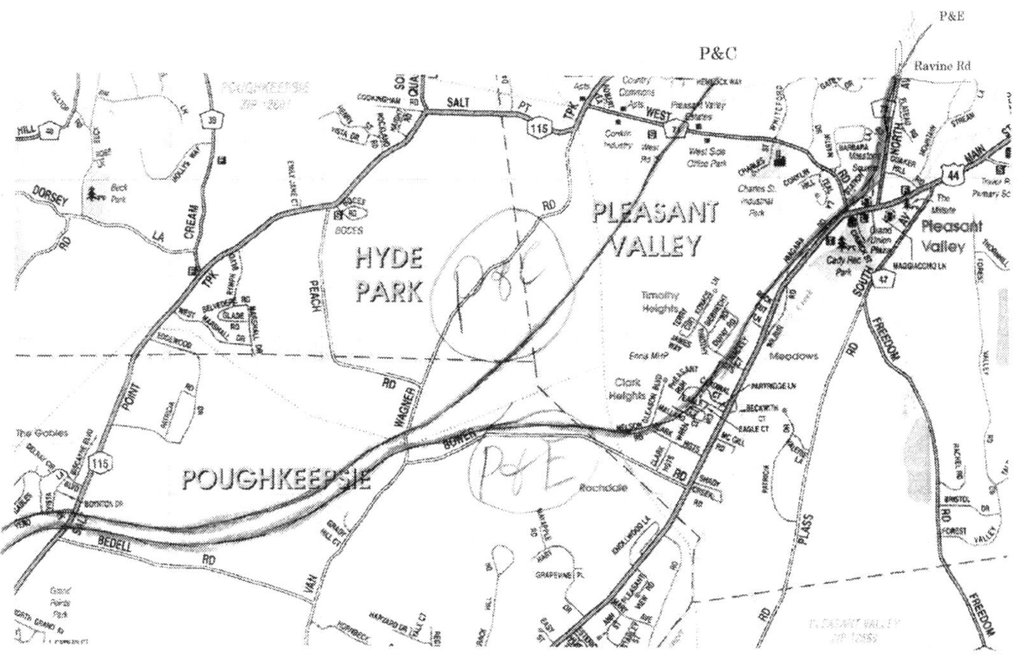

Map shows the path of the 2 railroads as they entered Pleasant Valley. (map from Bernie Rudberg)

As the train left the Smith Street yard in Poughkeepsie the tracks ran parallel until they got to the Van Wagner Station where they split until they got near Salt Point, where they crossed. (map next page)

Near the top right corner of this map where Ravine Road meets North Avenue, where the train track was is the road to Bower Park. That picture is on page 75 of this book.

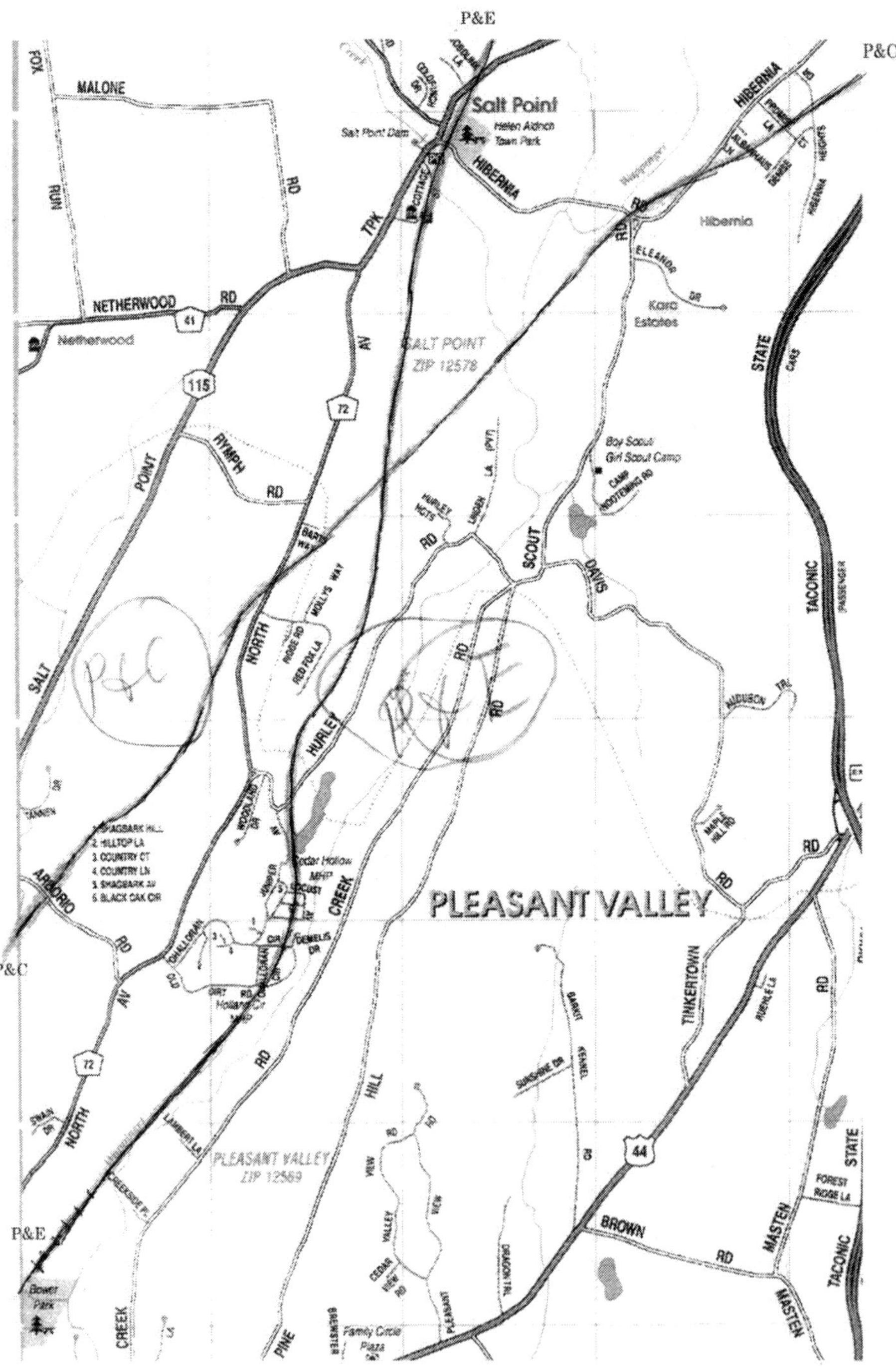

Map shows the path of the 2 railroads where they crossed near Salt Point.
(Map from Bernie Rudberg)

There was a station where the two tracks ran parallel and crossed Van Wagner Road near Bower Road. The station was called "Van Wagners" the place where the station was is now a Christmas tree farm called Fabulous Firs.

These smiling faces are waiting for the train at Van Wagners a few miles east of Poughkeepsie.
From the Roger Liller collection

This picture was taken from the edge of Van Wagner Road looking northeast toward Pleasant Valley.

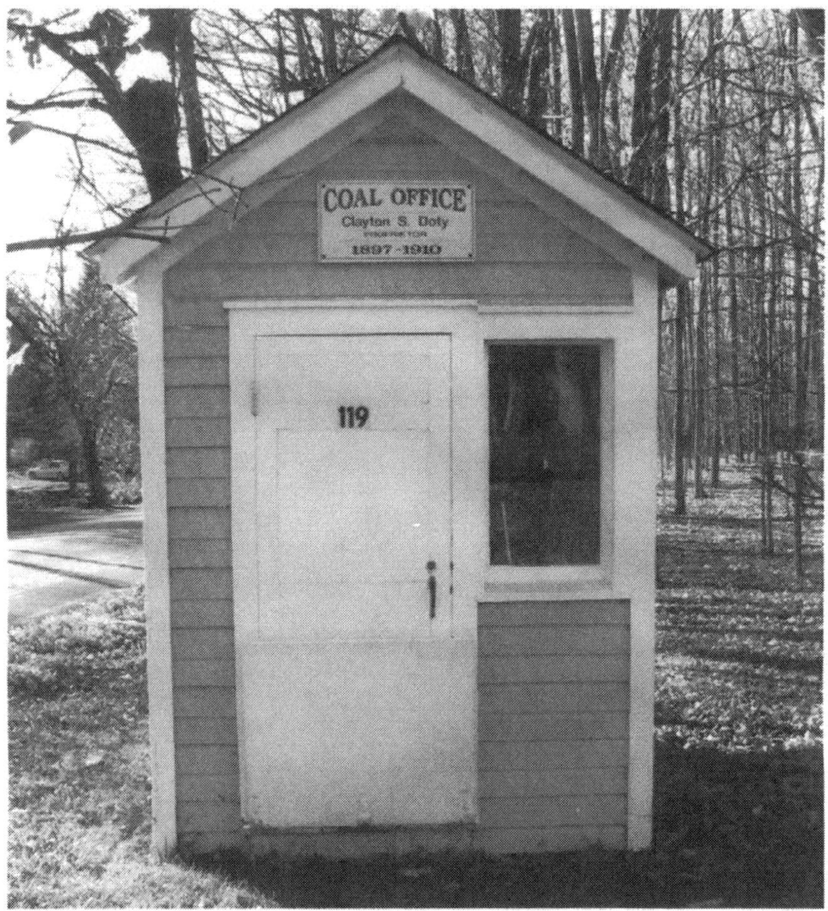

Doty's crossing coal office. B L Rudberg photo

This building still stands near the front of the Doty House, which Mrs. Olive still shares with her daughter.

When the P&C railroad was in full swing, people waited on the porches of the Doty house for the trains that rarely managed to be on time. In bad weather they spilled into the room with a bay window to stay warm and keep an eye out for the train.

The P&E railroad crossed North Avenue near what is now Ravine Road, and continued north toward Salt Point. What was the rail bed then is now the entry road to Bower Park.

By 1907 both lines had been consolidated into the CNE (Central New England) Railway. Shortly after the CNE gained control, a new rail connector was built in Pine Plains. This was a short S curve of tracks connecting the P&E to the P&C line to Silvernails, New York, near Pine Plains. After the connector was built the CNE abandoned the P&C line south of Pine Plains. The P&C had lasted barely twenty years from 1889 to 1909. During those years it changed owners many times.

The tracks are gone from the Pleasant Valley landscape but the memories remain. There are no more mills in Pleasant Valley, fewer farms, and the hotels are gone. To ride the train into New York City to work or shop a person must drive to the train station in Poughkeepsie.

The Salt Point station on a snowy day in February 1936.The station was where the Fire Station is now on Cottage Street.
Picture from the Roger Liller collection[m]

This P&E Wreck was on July 12, 1904 at Salt Point near the station.
Information and picture from the Roger Liller collection.

The freight train was waiting on the siding when a trainman named Kellerhouse was operating the switch. He mistakenly threw the switch the wrong way at the last second and put the passenger train on the same siding. After the crash Kellerhouse could not be found, the passenger train conductor, named Marcy, was taken to Vassar Hospital with a fractured skull.

The Civil War

Books written by some people might have referred to it as the "War Between The States"; books and new articles written at the time by northern authors, such as James H. Smith refer to it as "The War of the Rebellion." In school I learned it as the "Civil War."

February 4, 1861, the delegates of six of the seceding states, (South Carolina, Georgia, Alabama, Mississippi, Louisiana and Florida) met in convention at Montgomery, Alabama and formed a provisional government denominated "The Confederate States of America," founded as affirmed in the inaugural address of its president, on the principle of the inequality of men, and with human slavery as its corner-stone. Jefferson Davis was elected President and Alexander H. Stephens, Vice-President.

On the April 15, 1861, two days after the fall of Fort Sumter, President Lincoln called on the country for 75,000 men to suppress the uprising, which was then regarded, even by those in the best position to judge as a passing outbreak. These men were to be enlisted for three months. It was soon realized the south was serious and this was not to be a passing outbreak. In May, 1861, a call was issued for more men, to volunteer for three years. [n]

When during 1861 men were asked by President Abraham Lincoln to volunteer for service in the "War of the Rebellion," patriotic meetings were held around Dutchess County. One such meeting was held in Pleasant Valley, June 1, 1861.

> "June 1st a flag raising at Pleasant Valley was largely attended by people from all surrounding country to the number of three thousand or more. Ebenezer Allen was elected president. Several vice-presidents and secretaries were chosen. The Rev. F. B. Wheeler opened the exercises with prayer, after which addresses were delivered by Rev. B. F. Wile, James Bowne, Mayor of Poughkeepsie, Rev. F. B Wheeler, William Wilkinson, Esq., A. S. Pease and Hon. A. A. Nelson. The exercises were interspersed with music by the brass band."[o]

July 2, 1862 the President issued a call for volunteers to serve, because Pleasant Valley had a 1860 census population of 2,343, the quota expected was 76 men.[p] Many more than 76 men answered the call.

According to the Muster rolls from the New York State Archives, Albany, New York; Town Clerks' Registers of Men Who Served in the Civil War, ca 1861-1865; Collection Number: (N-Ar)13774; Box Number: 18; Roll Number 11, there were at least four men from Pleasant Valley: Charles Henry

Mastin, John Hart Mastin, Walter Smith, and Edmund Wolfew, who answered the call during the summer of 1861, and at least 148 more during the next four years. These records are hand written and sometimes hard to read or incomplete. I have done my best to check with other sources, such as the book History of Duchess County, New York by James H. Smith written in 1882, which provides a list of 134 names plus ten others unnamed, also various online sources including military rosters provided by individual regiment archives, The New York State Military Museum and Veterans Research Center on line, www.ancestery.com. Though my search was diligent, I cannot promise that no name is omitted or misspelled. The majority of the volunteers in 1862 joined the 128th Regiment or the 150th Regiment.

History of the one hundred and twenty-eighth regiment: New York volunteers (U.S. Infantry): in the late civil war by David Henry Hanaburgh, is a memoir of the 128th Regiment.

A Guide To Records Relating To The Civil War in the holdings of the New York State Archives, DRAFT, from The University of the State of New York, The State Education Department, Office of Cultural Education, State Archives and Records Administration, Albany, NY 12230, 1993. Lists 31 men from Pleasant Valley who volunteered for the 150th and 19 who volunteered for the128th Regiments in 1862.

I have put together as complete a list as possible at this time, for a total of over 150 names. See Appendix for list.

When extraordinary circumstances were encountered more details were sometimes available, some of those are listed here.

John Hart Mastin, 47th Artillery, was taken prisoner after taking part in eighteen battles, and died in Salisbury prison. (David Hanaburgh)

John Henry Smith, 128th Regiment, promoted to Cpl, died of chronic dysentery after the battle of Fort Hudson, in which he was engaged.

William. P. Smith, 128th Regiment, served in the Peninsula campaign, and after two years service was killed at Malvern Hill, July 1, 1863.

Peter G. Hemlett, unknown Regiment, was promoted to Hospital Steward, June 9, 1864.

Abram Turner, 128th Regiment, was taken prisoner October 19, 1864, at Cedar Creek and confined in Libby prison, was removed to Salisbury, North Carolina, paroled February 22, 1862, died at Pleasant Valley, New York, March, 1865. (David Hanaburgh)

Matthew Foster, 128th Regiment, was taken prisoner October 19, 1864, at Cedar Creek and confined in Libby prison, was removed to Salisbury, North Carolina, paroled February 22, 1865. (David Hanaburgh)

William H. Mackey (or McKay), 128th Regiment, was taken prisoner October 19, 1864, at Cedar Creek and confined in Libby prison, was removed to Salisbury, North Carolina, paroled February 22, 1865. (David Hanaburgh)

David Hanaburgh, 128th Regiment was taken prisoner October 19, 1864, at Cedar Creek and confined in Libby prison, was removed to Salisbury, North Carolina, paroled February 22, 1865. (David Hanaburgh)

William P. Smith, 128th Regiment, served in the Peninsula campaign, and after two years service was killed at Malvern Hill, July 1, 1863.

Daniel B. Ryder (or Rider), 128th Regiment Wounded May 27, 1863 at Port Hudson, Louisiana, died at Baton Rouge, Louisiana. (David Hanaburgh)

Walter P. Mastin, 150th Regiment, died of chronic dysentery at Fort Schuyler, immediately after the battle of Savannah.

Rowland Marshall, 150th Regiment, was promoted from private to 2nd Lieutenant, Sept. 1, 1862, and died at Georgetown, September, 1863.

Henry P. Williams, 150th Regiment from Pleasant Valley, after participating in the battles of Gettysburg, Ringgold, Atlanta and Black River Swamp, received a gunshot wound that went right through his body and lived to tell his tale at home in Pleasant Valley.

The 128th and 150th Regiments contained men from Pleasant Valley, New York:

The 128th Regiment New York Infantry was organized at Hudson, New York mustered[2] on September 4, 1862. The men from Pleasant Valley were mainly assigned to company D. The Regiment rendezvoused at Hudson, New York to serve for three years. The following day they left for Baltimore and sailed for New Orleans a few weeks later, aboard the transport *Argo*, along with three companies of the 114th Regiment Infantry to New Orleans. After nine days at sea in an overcrowded transport ship, on December 13th, they were quarantined because of measles at the Quarantine Station, 72 miles below New Orleans. "On December 22 nearly two hundred of the 128th were reported sick." [David Hanaburgh p. 14] Over the next months sickness ravaged the unit.

Spring of 1863 they were victorious at Port Hudson, Louisiana, a battle that lasted 48 days. David Hanaburgh noted in his book, on page 48, that on the 28th of May, after the battle of Port Hudson, an armistice was called to last until 2 p.m., during which permission was offered to carry off the wounded and to bury the dead. The dead were buried on the battle-field, the attack was not

[2] Muster: (verb) Assemble (troops), esp. for inspection or in preparation for battle

renewed during the day. There were other occasions documented by Hanaburgh of truces being called for medical and hospital supplies for comfort of the wounded of both armies.

The 128th Regiment New York Infantry organized at Hudson, New York and mustered in September 4, 1862.

SERVICE.—At Washington and Baltimore till December, 1862. Moved to New Orleans, La., and duty at Camps Parrapet and Kenner till March, 1863. Expedition to Ponchatoula March 20-May 15. Ponchatoula March 24-26. Barratara April 7. Gainesville April 18. Ponchatoula May 13. Camp Moore May 15. Moved to New Orleans, thence to Port Hudson, La., May 21-23. Siege of Port Hudson May 24-July 9. Assaults on Port Hudson May 27 and June 14. Surrender of Port Hudson July 9. Moved to Baton Rouge July 11, thence to Donaldsonville July 15. Duty there and at Baton Rouge till March, 1864. Red River Campaign March 23-May 22. Duty at Alexandria March 25-April 12. Grand Ecore April 13. Retreat to Alexandria April 21-26. Monett's Ferry, Cane River Crossing, April 23. Construction of dam at Alexandria April 30-May 10. Retreat to Morganza May 13-20. Mansura May 16. Expedition from Morganza to the Atchafalaya May 30-June 6. At Morganza till July 3. Moved to New Orleans, thence to Fortress Monroe, Va., and Washington, D. C., July 3-29. Sheridan's Shenandoah Valley Campaign August 7-November 28. Battle of Winchester September 19. Fisher's Hill September 22. Battle of Cedar Creek October 19. Duty at Kernstown and Winchester till January, 1865. Moved to Savannah, Ga., January 5-22, and duty there till March 5. Moved to Wilmington, N. C., March 5; thence to Morehead City, N. C., March 10. Moved to Goldsboro April 8, thence to Savannah May 2, and duty there till July. Mustered out at Savannah, Ga., July 12, 1865.

From A Compendium of the War of the Rebellion
by Frederick H. Dyer, page 1455

The 150th Regiment New York Infantry "Dutchess County Regiment" organized at Poughkeepsie, New York, mustered in October 10, 1862.

SERVICE.—Duty at Baltimore, Md., till February, 1863, and in the Middle Department till July, 1863. Joined Army of the Potomac in the field. Gettysburg (Pa.) Campaign July. Battle of Gettysburg, Pa., July 1-3. Pursuit of Lee July 5-24. Duty on line of the Rappahannock till September, 1863. Movement to Stevenson, Ala., September 24-October 3. Guard duty on line of the Nashville & Chattanooga Railroad till April, 1864. Atlanta (Ga.) Campaign May 1-September 8. Demonstration on Rocky Faced Ridge May 8-11. Battle of Resaca May 14-15. Near Cassville May 19. Advance on Dallas May 22-25. New Hope Church May 25. Battles about Dallas, New Hope Church and Allatoona Hills May 26-June 5. Operations about Marietta and against Kenesaw Mountain June 10-July 2. Pine Hill June 11-14. Lost Mountain June 15-17. Gilgal or Golgotha Church June 15. Muddy Creek June 17. Noyes Creek June 19. Kolb's Farm June 22. Assault on Kenesaw June 27. Ruff's Station, Smyrna Camp Ground, July 4. Chattahoochie River July 5-17. Peach Tree Creek July 19-20. Siege of Atlanta July 22-August 25. Operations at Chattahoochie River Bridge August 26-September 2. Occupation of Atlanta September 2-November 15. March to the sea November 15-December 10. Montieth Swamp December 9. Siege of Savannah December 10-21. Campaign of the Carolinas January to April, 1865. Averysboro, N. C., March 16. Battle of Bentonville March 19-21. Occupation of Goldsboro March 24. Advance on Raleigh April 9-13. Occupation of Raleigh April 14. Bennett's House April 26. Surrender of Johnston and his army. March to Washington, D. C., via Richmond, Va., April 29-May 19. Grand Review May 24. Mustered out at Washington, D. C., June 8, 1865. Veterans and Recruits transferred to 60th New York Infantry.

From A Compendium of the War of the Rebellion
by Frederick H. Dyer, page 1461

To show the sentiments of one of the Pleasant Valley residents here is a paper that was found in the Mill Site Museum.

"Transcribed from writing discovered on the back of a framed portrait of George Washington found in the 'attic' of Alson D. Van Wagner, Netherwood Road, Town of Pleasant Valley, New York, in September 1990. The framed portrait with glass on both sides presented to the historical collection of the Town of Pleasant Valley, Olive Doty, Town Historian, in December 1990. "

Following was written, the way it was written:

"1861

The year 1861 finds the American Republic in rather a bad situation -- Armed Rebels & Traitors are seeking to crush forever the glorious institutions founded by Washington & our Fathers. They have shelled Ft. Sumter & driven our Andrson out, "Stars & Stripes" -- The Capitol of the Republic is besided by armed Rebels, & if God does not protect it, it must fall. They have whipped our great army on the Bloody fields of Manasas whre we suffered an ignominous defeat -- Lexington (MO) has fallen a prey to Old Price. Old England's seaking for a quarl with us & every thing looks as though the Great Republic has seen her best days --

1862

600,000 brave men have called to the defence of our Country & flag. Our fleets cover the Ocean. The damed Rebels have been driven away from the Capitol -- The Stars & Stripes wave in tryumph over Manassas. All Misouri is swept clear of Rebels. Tennessee is restored to the Union. The Stars & Stripes wave on the Sacred Soil of South Carolina & on every other traitrous state save Texas. England is silenced let her come now if she dare! We can skin her like a cat. Old Mason & Slidell have been set free by our Hon Bill Seward. Curse their black hearts! Jeff Davis is on his last legs & the Rebelion is about busted.

Gilbert Williams

Pleas. Valley March 1862"

Pleasant Valley Society for the Detection of Horse Thieves

Records show that the Pleasant Valley Association for the Detection of Horse Thieves was in existence from at least 1811 to 1935.

This article appeared December 4, 1811, page 4 of the Poughkeepsie Journal and Constitutional Republican, it includes names of 52 members:

Horse Thieves

TAKE NOTICE.

THE Association of Pleafant Valley for detecting Horfe Thieves and bringing them to juftice, will meet at Efick Angell's Hotel on the firft Monday of December next, for the purpofe of choofing their Officers for the enfuing year.

John Beadle, Garret Adriance, William Ely, Bronfon French, Court Vanficklin, Peter Stringham, Thomas Casey, Caleb Martin, John Pearsall, Ifaac Jones, Henry Wheeler, George T. Brinckerhoff, Efick Angell, Nathaniel Lattin, David Palmer, Ifrael Dean, John I. Copeman, Paul Medough, Jofhua Barnes, Ahasuerus E. Peters, Zachariah Flagler, David Barnes, John A. Pells, Jofeph Thorn, jun. Ifaac Holmes, Jacob Manning, John Van Wagoner, Zachariah Van Wagoner, Jacob Oftrom, Aaron Carman, Stephen Augevine, Minard Viele, John C. Horton, Ifaac Forman, Eli Angevine, Jofeph Holmes, Daniel Oftrom, George Lomaree, Ifaac Travis, Thomas Casey, jun. Uriah Smith, Ifaac W. Balding, Robert Hallett, James Downs, Jofhua Collins, George Brown, John N. Van Wagoner, John Houghtalin, Solomon Van Wagoner, Richard I. Thorn, John Rogers, Benjamin Dubois.

WILLIAM ELY, *Clerk.*

Pleafant Valley, Nov. 9th, 1811. 72-4w

This article appeared December 22, 1813, Page 3, of the Poughkeepsie Journal and Constitutional Republican, it includes names of 67 members:

Horse Thieves,

TAKE NOTICE.

THE Pleasant Valley Association for the detection of Horse Thieves have had their annual meeting, and do hereby give notice to any thief or thieves who dare steal any horse or horses from either of the subscribers, that they have appointed a sufficient number of active riders who hold themselves in readiness at all times upon the shortest notice to pursue them with the utmost speed.

John Beadle, Garret Adriance, William Ely, Court Van Sicklen, Peter Stringham, Caleb Mastin, John Pearsall, Isaac Jones, Henry Wheeler, George Brinckerhoof, Eseck Angel, Nathaniel Lattin, David Palmer, Israel Dean, John I. Copeman, Joshua Barns, Ahasueras E. Peters, Zachariah Flagler, David Barns, John A. Pells, Joseph Thorn, Jun. Isaac Holmes, Jacob Manning, John Van Wagner, Zachariah Van Wagner, Jacob Ostrom, Aaron Carman, Stephen Angevine, Minard Viele, John C. Horton, Isaac Forman, Eli Angevine, Joseph Holmes, Daniel Ostrom, George Lummorce, Isaac Travis, Thomas Casey, Jr. Uriah Smith, Isaac W. Baldwin, Robert Halett, James Downs, Joshua Collins, John N. Van Wagner, John Hoghtolin, Richard I. Thorn, John Rogers, Benjamin Dubois, Thomas Broadway, George Flagler, Benjamin D. Hasbrook, Isaac Wiley, Thomas T. Carpenter, Thomas Gager, Josiah Ward, Joel Turrell, William Holmes, Zepheniah Churchill, Jacob H. Frost, Bartlet Marshall, William Golder, Isaac Allen, Abraham I. Conklin, Wheeler C. Holmes, Henry Peters, Jonathan Roberts, George H. Peters, and Silas Downing.

Clinton, Dec. 13th, 1813. 81-3w

A December 4, 1929 notice on page 10 of the Poughkeepsie Eagle News of the annual meeting shows that automobile thieves had been added to horse thieves as the object of detection:

> "**THIEVES CATCHERS MEET**
>
> The annual meeting of the Pleasant Valley society for Apprehension of Horse and Automobile Thieves was held at the Fire House Monday evening at 8 o'clock. This association formed more than half a century ago is still of the original few in existence in the country."

December 5, 1935, page 4, of the Poughkeepsie Eagle tells of the end of the Association.

HORSE THIEVES GROUP DECIDES TO DISBAND

The Pleasant Valley Horse Thieves association, an organization formed in 1870 for the prosecution of horse thieves, disbanded Monday night because there is no longer any horse stealing going on.

The association was said to be the last of its kind in New York state. The balance in the treasury of the organization will be distributed to the 25 members and each will receive a check for $5.20. Dues of the association were 25 cents annually and the initiation fee was $1. The books of the association will be turned over to the Pleasant Valley library.

At one time practically everybody in Pleasant Valley belonged to the association. A few years ago it stepped beyond the scope implied by its name and recovered a stolen automobile.

Copy of minutes of the final meeting of the Association:

Pleasant Valley NY Dec 2 1934-35

The annual meeting of the Pleasant Valley Hose Shops Assn was held in the Village Hall at 7 30 PM for the purpose of disbanding;

Treas Report Bal on Hand Dec 3 1932 = 114.11
Rect Dues 1933-34-35
Bank Bal Dec 2 11.61
Bal on Hand 125.72
Disb 1933-34-35

Moved Mr G S Masten be treasurer of the Hose Shops carried;

Moved we disband & divide the total money on hand Among the members in good standing & Record book be Placed in Free Library. Carried

Geo S House
Sect

The following are members

Chas Rossway	25	Thos Drake	25	Thos J Drake	25
Albert Husted	25	[illegible]	25	[illegible] Smith	25
Thos Masten	25	A [illegible]	25	Edw Drake	25
Ged House	25	HC Lawrence	25	H [illegible]	25
Lillie Knapp	25	A Smith	25	Mr G S Masten	25
Mrs G J Brown	25	Myron Smith	25	A Graham	25
Chas [illegible]	25	HDW Brown	25	J [illegible]	25
Fred Wallace	25	Sybil Brown	25		
Fred Barrett	25	[illegible]	25		

Each member received $5.20

Last and final page

On December 16, 1935, eleven days after the report of the disbanding of the Pleasant Valley association, the front page of the same paper carried a two column wide article stating that Upper Red Hook still had and anti-horse thief society, which was organized in 1796 and was still flourishing. At that time the group had 33 members, including 1 woman.

As of October 2, 1963 the Red Hook association was still active with reportedly sixty-five member attending the 166th annual meeting. Records at that time showed the group hadn't nabbed a horse thief since 1898, and only eight horses were owned by society members.

As of fall 2011 the Red Hook Society for the Apprehension and Detection of Horse Thieves is still in existence. Reportedly the records of the meetings from 1796 to 1940 have been digitized and are searchable by computer.

Pleasant Valley Post Office

"The Pleasant Valley Post Office was established on October 1, 1813, as reported in Frank Hasbrouck's "History of Dutchess County" in these words:

> "The Village (Pleasant Valley) becoming quite a manufacturing center and increasing in population, the inhabitants in 1813 petitioned the government for a post office, which was granted."

Amasa Angell was the first postmaster, but it seems that many months before he did transport Pleasant Valley mail from Poughkeepsie, because the official records of Gideon Granger, Postmaster General under President Thomas Jefferson on April 17, 1813 show the following entry:

> "Amasa Angell, Esqr., Pleasant Valley, N. Y.
>
> Sir:
>
> I have received yours of the 8th ult.[3] You are hereby authorized to transport a mail between your office & Poughkeepsie on every Wednesday for & on your own account and this letter is your authority for so doing.
>
> (signed) G.G."

Apparently Amasa Angell thereafter handled the mail between Pleasant Valley and Poughkeepsie. When Pleasant Valley received its own post office, he was the logical choice for the position of postmaster.

In the days almost two centuries ago, mail service was not a simple matter. Postage stamps did not yet exist, they did not come into use until 1847. Until then and for many years after postage was paid in cash and in most cases by the recipient of the letter. Postage rates were complicated, determined in each case by the number of sheets which a letter consisted of and distance which it had to travel. There were in effect 24 different letter rates and these rates were high, considering the purchase value of the dollar in those days. A single sheet letter within a 40 mile distance cost 8 cents and a four sheet letter, traveling over 500 miles, had a rate of $1.00, and these extremely

[3] Ultimo: adverb; definition in or of the month proceeding the current one. abbreviation: ult.

high charges were increased by 50% in 1815. Such rates put the mail service far beyond the means of the average citizen.

Following the example of Great Britain, lower and simplified postage rates were established in 1845, namely 5 cents for a single letter within 300 miles and 10 cents for delivery beyond 300 miles. In 1847 postage stamps were introduced and postage had to be prepaid by the sender. Beginning 1851 the rates varied from 3 cents to 40 cents and in 1863 postage was changed to 3 cents per half ounce. After several other changes, 2 cents became the standard rate in 1919 and subsequently was changed to 3 cents, 4 cents and finally to 5 cents on January 1, 1963.[9] There have been many changes to the structure and pricing of the postal rates over the years, as of January 22, 2012 the cost of mailing a one ounce letter within the United States is 45 cents and a postcard is 32 cents.

During the years of 1885 through 1914 the job of Postmaster switched from Edward C. Drake, a Republican, to Wright Devine, a Democrat, because the office alternated according to National Politics. Each man had a store, where the post office was located while he was postmaster.

Photo Courtesy of Andrew Hunt

Wright Devine's store and Post Office, date of picture unknown.

Wright Devine Store with Swastika Inn, circa 1912 (GBG)
(Until the Nazis used this symbol, the swastika was used by many cultures throughout the past 3,000 years to represent life, sun, power, strength, and good luck.[4])

Drake Store and Post Office, circa 1890 (MB)

[4] http://history1900s.about.com/cs/swastika/a/swastikahistory.htm June 11, 2012

Mr. Wright Devine had the post office in his store, on Main Street, with his residence adjoining the store on the east side. The store location, later a grocery store, is now a small strip mall. He was appointed Pleasant Valley postmaster July 17, 1885 to August 6, 1889, and again December 8, 1893 to November 16, 1897. As the politics changed, the postmasters changed.

Mr. Drake, also a merchant, had his store and the post office in the stone building north of the bridge. He lived in the Dr. Traver house, north of the store, along what is now Quaker Hill Road. He served as postmaster three different times with a total of 27 years service. Mrs. Drake was Annie E. Devine, a sister of Wright Devine, who followed Mr. Drake twice as postmaster. Mr. Drake was postmaster January 5, 1880 to July 16, 1885, August 7, 1889 to December 6, 1893, and November 17, 1897 to February 11, 1915.[r]

In the center is the well known building that served as the Post Office while Mr. Drake was Postmaster. It is currently the office of local Attorney Fred Schaefer.

During the mid 1930's the dark building in the center housed the Post Office.

In 1951 the Post Office moved to this building on Main Street next to the Valley Market. It remained there until these buildings were torn down to make way for new stores.

The right side of this building is the current Post Office, it has been in this building on Main Street since the previous one was torn down around 1971. The left side contains apartments. circa 2012 (PH)

The Sesquicentennial of the Post Office book also contains information on the Gretna Post Office:

"Nearly everyone looks forward to mail time. Rural delivery brings mail to a box by the side of the road each morning, but that isn't the way it was in the early history of our area.

In earlier days in the section of Gretna and Netherwood Roads, mail was picked up at the railroad station in Salt Point, from there it was brought to a farm kitchen, centrally located to serve the families in the nearby vicinity. The late Marquis Van de Water's farm seemed logical for this purpose because it was centrally located, families could come from several roads to collect their mail, this served as the Gretna Post Office. A pigeon-hole box hung on the wall where each family had a section for the deposit of their mail. Such familiar names as Dunn, Horton, Coles, and Van Wagner came for their mail at the Gretna Post Office. These neighborly calls to collect the mail enriched the lives of the families, and helped to create good community relations, especially where many folks lived in proximity to each other.

The late Mr. Walter Van Rensselaer was the mail carrier who brought the mail each day from Salt Point. His home at Netherwood served as the Netherwood Post Office. When rural free delivery came into effect, Mr. Van Rensselaer was the mail carrier from Salt Point. His daily trip with a black horse that was blind, and a two-wheeled sulky wagon was a familiar sight which everyone looked forward to each day."[5]

Pleasant Valley Fire Department

In early 1903, Alfred Leith, Foreman of the John Knott Fire Company, offered the services of the organizations to the Village Board of Pleasant Valley furnish fire protection. The services were accepted in 1903, and reaccepted in 1907. In 1913, the company became known as the Pleasant Valley Volunteer Fire Company. On June 1, 1913, the company leased Pleasant Valley Hall (Lovelace Hall) next to the Pleasant Valley Grill for monthly fire meetings. Included in the rental was the use of a small building in the rear for fire equipment "and necessary repairs." The large building became known as "Firemen's Hall" and was used as such until 1922, when a new two-story concrete block building was erected, just west of "Firemen's Hall."

Fireman's Hall c 1900(GBG)

Postcard of Lovelace's Hall (GBG)

The concrete block building erected in 1922 as the Pleasant Valley Firehouse (GBG)

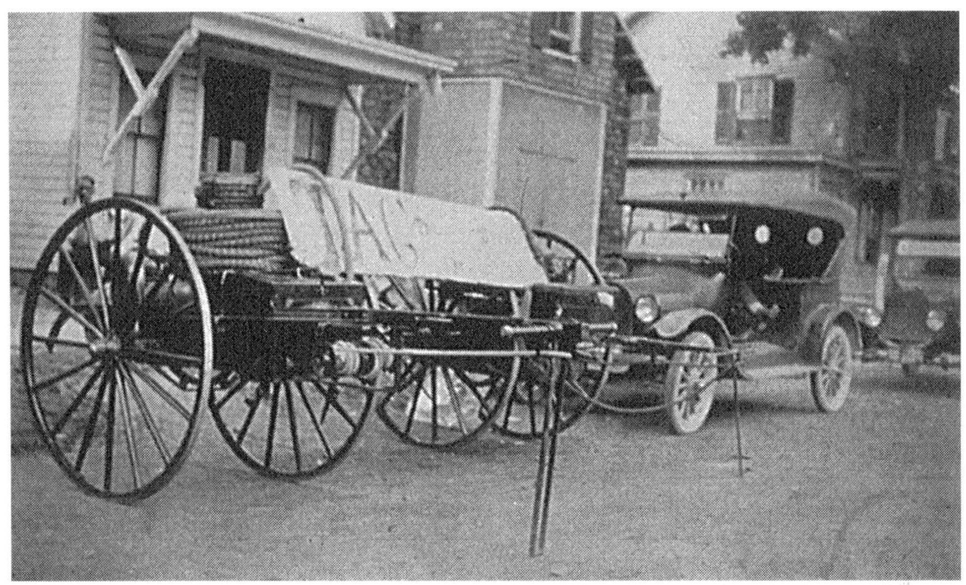

In 1925, the Village Board voted to replace two two-wheeled 55 gallon chemical "wagons", pulled by four to six men per apparatus. (GBG)

In March 1926, a new Mack combination pumper, hose, ladder and chemical apparatus was delivered. In 1928, the Pleasant Valley Fire District #1, which included the whole township, was formed, due to previous dis-incorporation of the village. In 1937, another Mack apparatus was purchased, requiring additional apparatus room. (GBG)

Another view of the first firehouse on Main Street. (MB)

Firemen in action, South Avenue, taken by George Masten. Circa 1927 (MB)

The second Firehouse on Main Street. (GBG)

In 1941, a new concrete block building was dedicated on Main Street next to the Methodist Church, and was used until the flood of 1955, at which time it was condemned. In 1950, a new Ward LaFrance was purchased and delivered in 1951. During the same year, an emergency first aid squad was formed, and a new Ford ambulance placed in service for "all residents of the fire district."

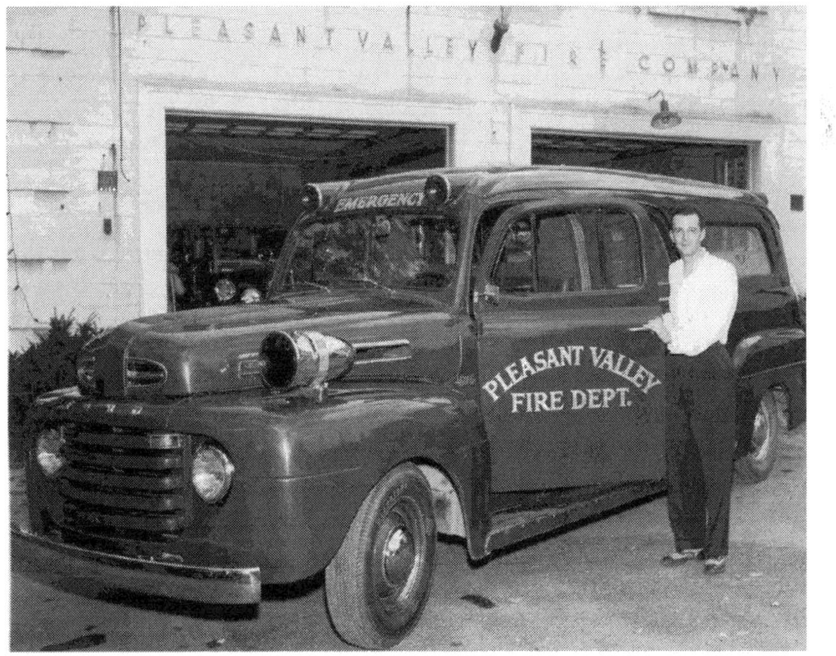

Don Carroll with Pleasant Valley's first ambulance. (PC)

A Poughkeepsie New Yorker article from 1941 found in the Pleasant Valley historical files contained the following picture and information:

Pleasant Valley dedicated its new modern firehouse Saturday. Twelve county companies took part in the ceremonies, which included a parade and an informal speaking program. The Pleasant Valley firemen below aided the program.

Poughkeepsie New Yorker Photos

Pleasant Valley Dedicates New Firehouse

Front row, left to right, William Millard, Joseph Silvernail, Archie Smith, Reginald Cary, William Hilliker, John Donegan.

Back row, left to right Albert Lawson, Lester Phillips, chairman of the board of commissioners, Harold Cady, Fred Ruehle; commissioner, DuBois Haight; chief.

In 1946 a group of men from Salt Point petitioned the Board of Fire Commissioners for permission to form a company in their village, to be known as Salt Point Fire Company. They formed in 1947, using the old railway station as their headquarters, and a homemade apparatus for fire fighting. In 1950 a used pumper was purchased for Salt Point, and after repairs and painting placed in service. In 1955 a new one story concrete block building was erected for the Salt Point Company, to replace the old railroad station. Having more than one company, we qualified as a Fire Department. In 1960, a new Ford ambulance was purchased and placed in service, replacing the older equipment. In 1961, two new ford pumpers were purchased, one being delivered to Pleasant Valley and one to Salt Point in 1962.

The third Pleasant Valley Firehouse on Main Street was torn down to become the driveway to the new firehouse. Circa 1955 (GBG)

The fourth and current Pleasant Valley Firehouse on Main Street. (TS)

During the 1940's or 1950's the Fire Department held Minstrels as fundraisers. Over the years the Minstrels have been discontinued, because they were considered offensive.

ANNUAL

MINSTREL & DANCE

PLEASANT VALLEY FIRE CO.

Friday, March 28, 1941

At the Pleasant Valley School Auditorium

Above is the cover of the program of one of the Minstrel Shows(PH)

Several men on the end of each row would be in "black-face", they would get up during the show and tell jokes or sing.(PamC)

Chorus

Clifford Allen	Eddie Smith
John Reid	Alden Traver
John Freeman	Kenneth Budd
Francis Stevenson	Howard Amstead
Irving Bower	Theodore Traver
Lorenzo Williams	George Cady
James E. Clark	Frank Lasko
Kenneth Sherow	Irving Parks
Reginald Cary	Norman Bennett
Bill Agne	Richard Traver

Don Robison

THE PLEASANT VALLEY FIRE CO.

Wish to express their appreciation to all members of the cast and the committees for their untiring efforts in making this production a success. We also thank those who contributed in any way and those who are here to view this performance.

Please patronize our advertisers.

Program

Interlocutor—GEORGE C. CLARK

I OPENING NUMBER - Medley - *Chorus*

II END SONG - Nobody - *Sherman Bennett*

III SPECIALTY - Harmonica Trio - *Traver Boys*

- Guitar Accompanist - *Don Robison*

IV END SONG - Dark Town Strutters Ball - *Donald T. Clearwater*

V SPECIALTY - Guitar - *Don Robison*

- Goin' Back to Texas - "

VI END SONG - I Wasn't Scared - *George Tyrell*

VII SPECIALTY - Scotch Novelty - *John Hennessey*

- She's The Lass For Me - "

VIII SPOON NOVELTY *George Tyrell*

IX SOLO - Ida - *Jack Cavo*

X END SONG -If You've Got A Little Bit- *Chet Duncan*

XI DANCE TEAM *Bobby Baker, Jane Kaman*

XII SOLO -In The Town Where I Was Born- *Karl Roider*

XIII MAGICAL INTERLUDE *Bernard G. Schamberg*

XIV SOLO -Where Did You Get That Hat- *Jack Howe*

XV SPECIALTY - Dances - *George Tyrell, Chet Duncan*

XVI CLOSING NUMBER -God Bless America- *Chorus*

Bill Corey - At The Piano

Over the years the firemen had many baseball teams.

Date could be 1940's, Photographer unknown

Front row, left to right, Frank Stoutenburg, Orlando VanWagner, John Toth, Harold Cady, Potsy Ferguson, Ed Silvernail, Chet Carlson.
Back row, left to right, Howard Amsted, Frank Millard, Bill Brown, Jim Millard, Warner Parks, Ed Carlson, Bill Silvernail

Date could be 1950's, Photographer unknown

Front row, left to right, Jimmy Decker, Johnnie Decker, Mike Cady, (boy in front is Stevie Decker), Joe Roberts, Custer "Catzi" Pultz.
Back row, left to right, Merritt "Mickey" Embree, Bill Silvernail, Orlando VanWagner, Doug Eighmie, Nelson Freer, Jack Moorehead, Gene Pultz.

Apartment house fire, March 1, 1953 (HMJ)

According to the Poughkeepsie Journal of March 2, 1953, four families were left homeless when this 32 room, 2 ½ floor apartment house on South Avenue burned. Before being an apartment house this building was a boarding house for mill workers.

Former Chief Cady said he was watching television, when suddenly he saw Mrs. Decker run past a window, he ran outside, she was waving her hands and shouting fire, she told him the oil stove in her home had exploded. He called the firemen. Meanwhile other occupants were carrying there furniture and personal articles from the building. When the firemen arrived they helped save the furnishings, and fought the blaze. George Cady Sr. whose home was destroyed, received a cut of the right hand, he said he was injured as he carried some of his belongings from his home.

Occupants of the apartment house were former fire chief and Mrs. George S. Cady Sr., and their daughter, Carol Ann; Mr. and Mrs. Freeman Decker, Mr. and Mrs. Phillip Scully and their three children and Mrs. Ada Burdick. The owner of the building was Garcia T. DuBois, Main Street, Pleasant Valley.

County mutual aid from Salt Point Fire Company and companies from Rochdale and Arlington prevented other homes and buildings from burning, about 100 volunteer firemen from four companies fought the flames for more than 2 hours. The loss was reported as upwards of $15,000.

Schools in Pleasant Valley

Below is a 1867 Beers map showing the lines for the 12 school districts in Pleasant Valley.

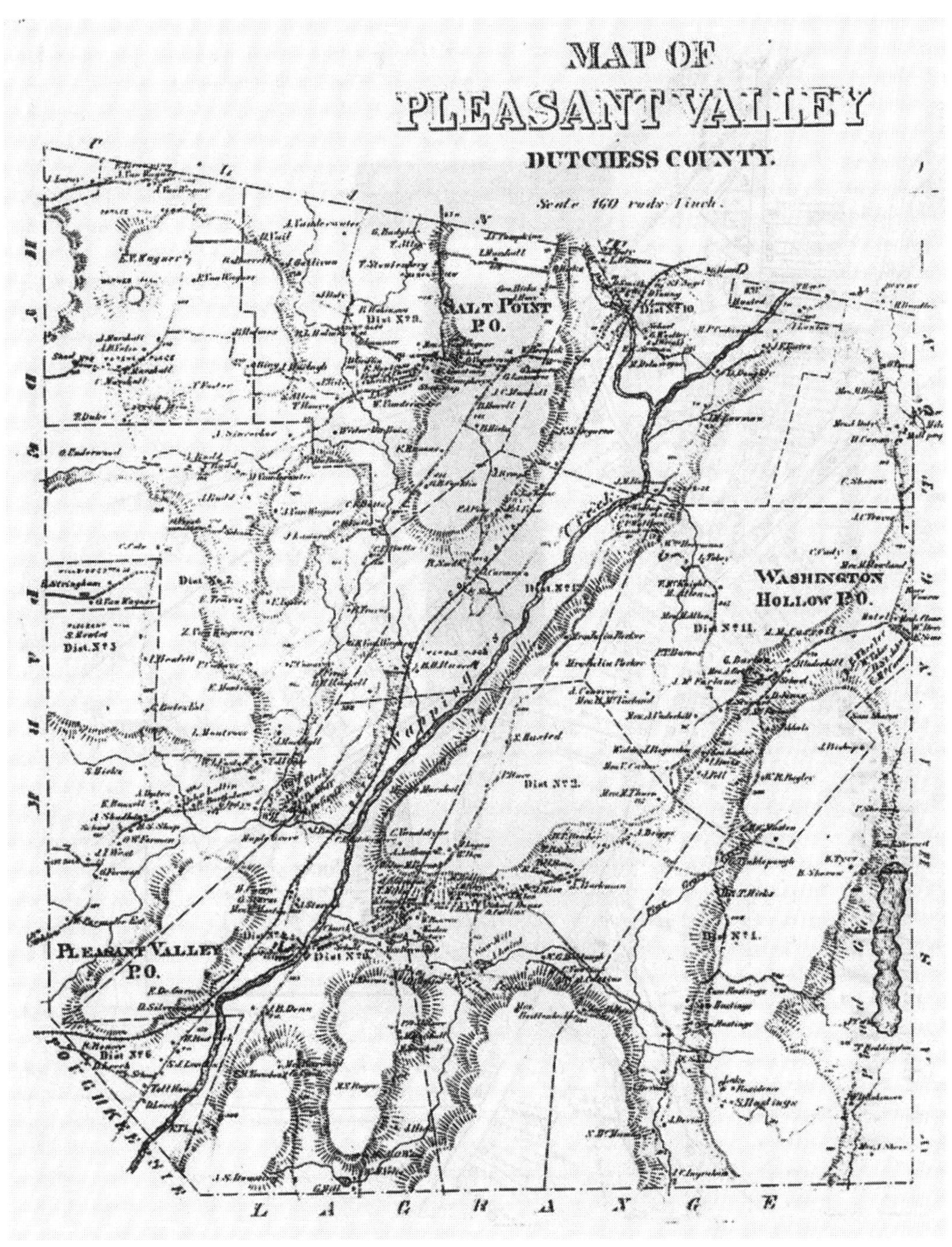

From memories of Olive Doty, town historian and Pleasant Valley Native:

> "There were twelve school districts in the town once the state law was established. The Beers map of 1867 shows these districts. Trustees were elected for each of these districts. Elections were held and the schools were governed by the elected trustees according to the guidelines set by the state board of regents.
>
> Early on they were one room school buildings with outhouses, one for boys and one for girls and in most cases water had to be carried from the nearest farm house. No transportation was provided and the teachers were boarded generally by one of the trustees. Schools were built in a two mile radius.
>
> The New York State Regents exams for the grades were only given in the town in the hamlet of Pleasant Valley at Traver Road School. A lady told me that she took the train from Salt Point to take her exams.
>
> When students graduated from grade school and wished to continue their education they either had to go to a private boarding school in Poughkeepsie or to Poughkeepsie High School. Some of these students commuted by Masten's bus or by the railroads. The early records of the P&E Railroad show that laundry boxes were sent home for the clothes to be washed and ironed by Mama."

The bus that you might have taken to school in Poughkeepsie.

The history of Pleasant Valley schools as told by Dorothy E. Albertson, Principal, Pleasant Valley School, reported in the "Valley Bulletin" of March 20, 1968, page 15:

> "The first school in Pleasant Valley was built in the early 1800's - about 1830 - with all grades attending. This structure was a one room building located on the upper corner of our present school property. It embodied all the characteristics of the one room country school house - all its problems - its delights and challenges. The large wood stove in the center of the room - "thoroughly warmed" those near it - those farther away froze. There was another one room school located in North Avenue and several scattered throughout the present Pleasant Valley School District. We are told there was much rivalry between the North Avenue rural school and the one on the present Pleasant Valley School property.

> In 1904 the building here was torn down and a short time later a modern four room wooden building was erected. In the beginning grades 1 - 4 were in one room while grades 5 - 8 were in another. The remaining two rooms were not used at first. Pupils from the surrounding rural schools were brought in to the Pleasant Valley School to take the Regents examinations."
>
> "In approximately 1922 the area had grown so that the four rooms were all in use. Pleasant Valley was not as yet a part of the Arlington School District."

In 1928 at Pleasant Valley School, Mrs. Marion Carroll taught 1st and 2nd grades, Mrs. Ruth Bachedler Howland taught 3rd and 4th grades, Mrs. Margaret Dean Clark taught 5th and 6th grades, and Mr. Harold Storm taught 7th and 8th grades. Then with consolidation, Pleasant Valley became part of District #7 in 1931. In the autumn of 1931 Mr. Harold C. Storm was promoted to Principal of the Elementary Grades of Arlington and Pleasant Valley. He held this position until June 1936 when he resigned to take a position as Superintendent in Putnam County. [t]

Miss Albertson goes on in the April 3, 1968 edition of the Valley Bulletin page 11 & 12, to tell that wood from the four-room school building was given to the Town of Pleasant Valley by District vote and used for the construction of Pleasant Valley's Free Library building. Records show that all the school children participated in a fitting parade and ceremony at this time. In 1944 she started teaching; in 1946 she began her job as full-time principal at Traver Road School. [u]After 38 years first teaching, then as principle of the Pleasant Valley School at Traver Road, Miss Dorothy E. Albertson retired.

The first Traver Road School from 1830 to 1904

The four room school on Traver Road, from 1904 until new school built.

The current school at Traver Road was built in 1933, the cornerstone of this school was laid by the Masons of Shekomeko Lodge according to the ancient customs of the craft. The first addition was built 1938, over the years many additions have been made. The school currently houses grades Kindergarten to second grade.

West Road/ D'Aquannis Intermediate School houses grades three to five. circa 2012, (TeddiS)

The students of Pleasant Valley School at Traver Road. with Professor Dumond. Date of Photo about 1910.

The Professor, the back row second from end right side, was a Civil war veteran who had lost an arm in battle.

Pleasant Valley School at Traver Road, grades 5, 6, 7, 8
picture taken October 17, 1919.

<u>Bottom row:</u> Walter Chamberlain, John Cuff, Donald Drake, George Gattea, Herbert Oakley, Floyd Masten, Lloyd Roberts, Herbert Tintle, Esmond Edwards

<u>Middle row:</u> Marcella McGrath, Avita Briggs, Ellen Teator, Florence Lovelace, Esther Coy, Massie Edwards, Kathleen Tompkins, Grace VanAlstyne, John Trotney

<u>Top row:</u> Lois Masten, Teacher-Mrs. Leona Bradley, Emilie Skidmore, Irene House, Celestine Crucius, Irva Briggs, DuBois Haight, Howard Amstead, George Myers.

Traver Road School class of 1930

Front row: Pete VanVlack, Lois Oakley, Betty Cosnick, Ruth Gillette, Morris Cady

Back row: Billy Silvernail, Irma Brown, Ida Peters, Della Seldridge, Janet Freeman, Florence Rogers, Marion Brown, Alice Gilbert, Ethella Bolce, Harny Nauta

Clifford Buck walking to the District #9 school during the late 1800's.

District #9 students with teacher.

District #10 Salt Point Class, 1920's E. Rozell, Teacher

District #10 class, 1800's DeLavergne image

District # 10; Hibernia Road, Salt Point School Mid 1800's

District # 10; Hibernia Road, Salt Point School circa 1960

Pleasant Valley Free Library

Pleasant Valleys first library, circa 1903

August 27, 1903, the first public library in Pleasant Valley opened its doors. It was located in a small building on Main Street between the former residence of Mrs. Frank Knapp and the present site of Allen Funeral Home. (That would be east of Allen's, it is currently the site of a bank.) There were 297 bound books on the shelves and the first day 21 books were in circulation. Mrs. Louis Schneider was acting librarian.

The Library Association was formed on May 8, 1903 at the home of J. Horton, which later became the Pleasant Valley Hotel. The following were chosen as trustees: H. N. W. Magill, President; Mrs. Louis Schneider, Secretary; C. Niver, Mrs. Frank Knapp and Mrs. Maud Husted, Treasurer.

On June 5, 1903 a temporary charter was applied for at the New York State Board of regents and constitution adopted. The first annual meeting was held at the home of Mrs. Frank Knapp on July 1, 1904.

In March 1905, a building lot at the corner of South Avenue and Main Street was presented to the Association. Application was made to the Board of

Regents for a permanent charter which was granted on June 29, 1905. A building committee was appointed consisting of Clarence Drake, Rev. R. R. Upjohn, Chester Husted and H. N. W. Magill. Ground was broken in August 1909 and the cornerstone laid with ceremony October 9, 1909, which included a parade of school children and interested citizens. The new building was opened for circulation of books on August 27, 1910. In the visitor's book the first autograph is Franklin D. Roosevelt, April 7, 1911. At the time he was a boy and was visiting the library with his class.

In 1912, two years after the new building had been opened, the old library building was destroyed by fire at 3 A.M. on Thanksgiving Day.

In 1918, the Library sponsored a supplementary school library at the local school. The Library was also the center for community carol singing during the Christmas season.

The Library has served as the Red Cross sewing center during both World War I and World War II, and served as a center for book collections to be sent to men and women in the service during that time.

Records show that the Dutchess County Historical Society was founded in the Pleasant Valley Library, on April 28, 1914.

The early Librarians were:

Mrs. Louis Schneider from August to December 1903

Nadine Magill from January 1904 to 1905

Mrs. Harry Magill (date not known)

Hattie Wolven held the position until 1919

Miss Marcia DuMond was appointed until 1928

Mrs. John Carson (later Mrs. Irving VanWert) served 1928 to 1938

Miss Grace DuMond forced to resign on account of ill health in 1953, She became librarian emeritus.

Mrs. Kenneth Sherow is the last recorded librarian at the library on South Avenue.

In 1953 the library hours were increased from eight hours a week to twelve hours a week to comply with state regulations. The circulations increased from twenty-one books the first day, to a ninety-one daily average with over five thousand volumes on the shelves, as compared to two hundred ninety-seven volumes when opened.

The second library at the corner of Main Street and South Avenue, circa 1954.

Inside of the second library was a very cozy place.

The library had a special little table for children to sit at.

Current Library, date unknown.

In February 1975, the Presbyterian manse became the new Pleasant Valley Free Library.

As of 2012, the library is open from 10:00 am to 8:30 pm Monday thru Thursday, 1:00 pm to 6:00 pm on Friday, 10:00 am to 4:00 pm on Saturday and is only closed on Sundays.

In addition to the library's large collection of books, CDs and DVDs, the library offers computer, fax, photocopier services, and free Wi-Fi for individuals with library cards. The library also provides help finding jobs and developing your career through the Dutchess County Job Resource Center, there are afternoon and evening book groups and monthly meditation groups.[v]

Pleasant Valley Hotel

The building on the south side of Main Street, in the center of town, that stood for almost 100 years was once a school. The Pleasant Valley Institute was established in 1876, as a boarding school for young ladies. According to the brochure boys who attended did so only as day students.

Pleasant Valley Institute.

BOARDING AND DAY SCHOOL

FOR YOUNG LADIES.

(Young Men taken as Day Scholars only.)

PLEASANT VALLEY, DUTCHESS CO., N. Y.

MRS. O. M. C. HOLMAN, PRINCIPAL.
MISS A. E. HOLMAN, ASSISTANT.

1876-77.

The Quarters begin Sept. 18th, Nov. 27th, Feb. 5th, and April 16th.

The course of study listed was quite complete, students completing the program would be well rounded.

Pleasant Valley Institute.

This Institute is located in Pleasant Valley, Dutchess County, N. Y., a healthy and delightful Village on the line of the Poughkeepsie, Hartford and Boston Railroad, seven miles from Poughkeepsie.

Everything about the establishment is perfectly adapted to securing the comfort and health of Pupils,—such as good water, a uniform degree of heat, and healthfully prepared food.

Boarding Pupils will be under the direct control of the Principal.

COURSE OF STUDY.

PRIMARY DEPARTMENT.—Reading, Writing, Spelling, Mental and Practical Arithmetic, Elementary Geography, and Science of Common Things.

ADVANCED DEPARTMENT.—Arithmetic, Geography, United States History, English Grammar, Natural Philosophy, Physiology, Chemistry, Rhetoric, Botany, Astronomy, Algebra and Geometry.

LANGUAGES.—French, Latin and German.

TERMS.

Board, Washing, Light, and Furnished Room,	per week,	$4.50
Week Boarders,	" " " " "	3.00
Primary Department, - - -	per Quarter,	5.00
Advanced Department, - - -	"	10.00
French Class Session, - - -	"	2.50
Latin " " - - -	"	2.50
German " " - - -	"	2.50
Single Pupil in French, Latin or German, -	"	5.00
Piano, Organ or Melodeon, - -	"	10.00
Vocal Music, - - - - -	"	2.50
Use of Instrument, - - - -	"	2.00
Pencil Drawing, - - - -	"	2.50

Ornamental Penmanship,

Painting in Oil or Water Colors.

Wax Flowers.

Pew Rent, same as charged in church.

Stationery and Books furnished at the Institute, at retail prices.

No deduction for absence, except in case of protracted sickness of pupils.

The above rates are payable in advance.

For further information, address

W. W. ARNOLD,
Pleasant Valley, Dutchess Co., N. Y.

In 1897 the building became a boarding house run by Franklin Knapp.

At one time, the hotel, called Clarkson House was owned by the Clarkson family, an English family. The master of the house always wore a high silk hat to Church, attending Sunday Services at St. Paul's Episcopal Church each week. He was taken to and from services in a carriage with a high seat in front and driven by a Negro coachman.

In the Clarkson home there were gas lights, signal bells connecting each room with the kitchen, a water tank in the attic which furnished water throughout the house, two hot air furnaces and a pipe organ.

May 1914, it was opened as the Swastika[5] Inn, by Mr. & Mrs. M. L. Koebel. Local newspaper reports it opening as a home-like hotel ready for the boarding season. At that time it was greatly modernized in many ways, being the first building in Pleasant Valley to have electric lights. At that time the Inn did not have a bar.

[5] Until the Nazis used this symbol, the swastika was used by many cultures throughout the past 3,000 years to represent life, sun, power, strength, and good luck. http://history1900s.about.com/cs/swastika/a/swastikahistory.htm June 11, 2012

During the 1920's while it was called the Swastika Inn, it was generally closed during the winters while the owners went to Florida, and re-opened in the spring for the busy tourist season.

Swastika Inn, circa 1920's

The tennis court in the rear of the Swastika Inn.

May 1929, the hotel was opened as Garrison Hall by Mrs. M. L. Koebel and her sister Mrs. Lotta M. Briggs. In 1942 it was known as the Clairmont Hotel, then Fitzpatrick's. In 1944 when it was Fitzpatrick's it was white with forest green trim.

Fitzpatrick Hotel Postcard, circa 1945

Fitzpatrick Hotel, circa 1948

It later became the Pleasant Valley Hotel, and was run by Mike Cady, the fire chief. During that time most of the local people referred to it as "Cady's."

Cady's Pleasant Valley Hotel, circa 1971

Back view of Cady's Pleasant Valley Hotel, circa 1971

In 1972, it was torn down to make way for a strip mall. The strip mall is still there today.

Talbot's

Talbots was a three-story frame structure, about 60 feet along the front. It was erected in 1770, and used as a private residence. In June 1814 it was mentioned in an advertisement for a "Fashionable Tailor" who opened a business nearly opposite the Flagler Hotel.

Arthur W. Bower, a local youth at the time recorded a special celebration, in his diary, that took place at Flagler's Hotel on June 12, 1865, the occasion being "*A welcome home for the 150th N.Y. S. V., the Dutchess County Regiment. The Regiment was well received and honored and a well filled table was spread*". In his diary he also mentions the Flagler's Hotel was noted for fine hospitality throughout the county as early as 1814.

Stephen E. Flagler hosted two anti-slavery meetings that we have records of, one in fall 1838 and the other, April 22, 1839. The Pleasant Valley Anti-Slavery Society was founded and also held its first anniversary meeting at Flagler's Hotel. Both men and women attended.

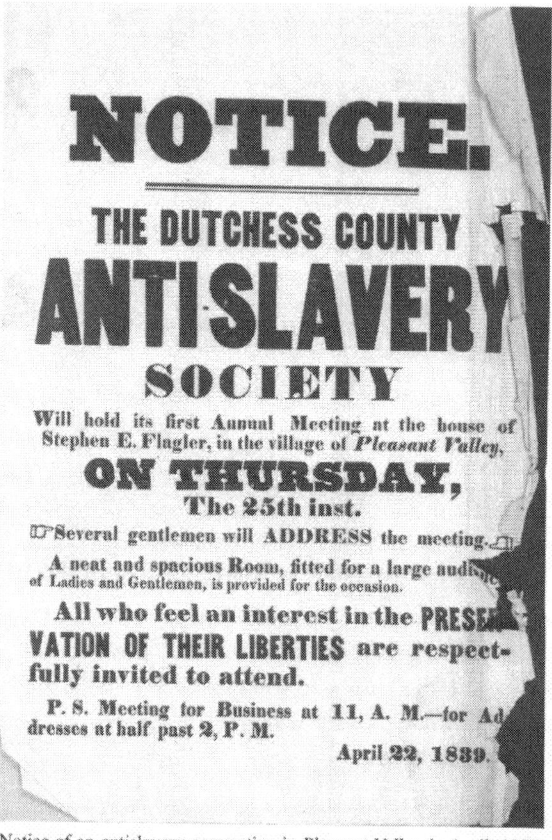
NOTICE.

THE DUTCHESS COUNTY

ANTI-SLAVERY

SOCIETY

Will hold its first Annual Meeting at the house of Stephen E. Flagler, in the village of *Pleasant Valley*,

ON THURSDAY,

The 25th inst.

☞Several gentlemen will ADDRESS the meeting.☜

A neat and spacious Room, fitted for a large audience of Ladies and Gentlemen, is provided for the occasion.

All who feel an interest in the PRESERVATION OF THEIR LIBERTIES are respectfully invited to attend.

P. S. Meeting for Business at 11, A. M.—for Addresses at half past 2, P. M.

April 22, 1839.

Notice of an antislavery convention in Pleasant Valley in April, 1839. Dutchess County Antislavery Society, Manuscripts and Archives Division, The New York Public Library, Astor, Lenox and Tilden Foundations.

The hotel remained in the Flagler family until October 16, 1865 when it was sold to W. C. Armstrong. In December of 1884 the hotel burned and was rebuilt by Mr. Armstrong. It was operated by Armstrong from 1865 to 1898.

William C. Armstrong portrait, Armstrong family and servants both, circa 1870 (GBG)

Armstrong Hotel (GBG)

There was a building in front of the hotel where medicine shows were held in the early 1900’s, after that building was torn down, croquet games were played on the park-like front lawn of the hotel.

The old hotel burned while Mr. Armstrong owned it but it was rebuilt on the same site.

Hoctor's Hotel from a postcard circa 1906 (GBG)

From 1898 to 1912 the Hotel was owned by Michael Hoctor. There was a building behind the hotel in 1902, where Catholic mass was held before St. Stanislaus Catholic church was built.

Barth's Hotel, unknown date (GBG)

In 1926 it became Barth's. In 1944 it still had large lawns in front and along the side. It was cream color with green trim and porch along the front. In the winter there was an area of the side yard that sometimes flooded and froze to make a skating rink for the local kids.

The interior of Barth's, this was referred to as the Log Cabin Grill.

After Barth's, from 1951 to 1982 it was owned by James and Mable Talbot, when they died, it was run by their son and his wife Mike Talbot and Ann Cameron Talbot. During that time the name was Talbot's Hotel.

Talbot's Inn, circa 1960 (GBG)

Talbot's Hotel as it looked when planning meetings for Pleasant Valley's 150th Anniversary celebration were held there in 1971. (GBG)

During the 1980's the hotel was rented first to Harry Maronus who change the name to the 1830 Inn and later to Eileen Cudney, who changed the name to the 1830 Steak House.

Front and side view of the 1830 Steak House, circa 1989 (GBG)

Rear of the 1830 Steak House, circa 1989 (GBG)

The 1830 Steak House in the process of being demolished to make way for the Mile Stone Square Plaza.

No history of this hotel would be complete without this additional information furnished by lifelong Pleasant Valley resident and local historian, Olive Doty.

Remembering the 1830 Inn

By Olive Doty, written 1995

The corner of Route #44 and North Avenue in the hamlet of Pleasant Valley, N. Y. is fondly remembered as the location of the "1830 Inn". Although through the years, from 1830 to1984, it went by other names, until its final demise.

The first person to have an inn on that location was George W. Wood who purchased two plots in 1826. The first consisting of 53 acres and the second, 21 acres. This amount of land remained the same until 1912 when it was purchased by Leonard Carpenter at which time the acreage had been reduced to 7.68 acres. Then, when it was purchased by Walter and Anne E. Barth, the acreage had been further reduced to 2.51 acres and remained the same through 1984. (See Chronology on Page 148)

We don't know much about the owners themselves until it was purchased by W. C. Armstrong in 1865. According to a biography appearing in J. H. Beer's Commenmorative Biography, published in 1897, Mr. Armstrong was born in New York City in 1830 and educated there as an engineer. He went to Cuba with bibles, presumably to sell to the natives. He remained there for nine years running a sugar plantation and then returned to New York City with a large consignment of cigars to sell. The account goes on to say that he was a man of comprehensive business powers.

He remained the owner of what he called "Pleasant Valley Hotel" for 33 years. During that time, he and his second wife had two daughters, one of which married George Rutherford, a music teacher and dealer in music in Poughkeepsie. With his wife, Bessie Clayton Armstrong, playing piano, Mr. Rutherford taught ballroom dancing at the inn. The Rutherford School of Dance, established in later years in Poughkeepsie has many fine pieces of furniture that came from the inn.

Mr. Armstrong had a dock on the mill pond by the bridge, that offered his guests boating, fishing and access to a picnic area.

The original building was destroyed by fire in 1884 in spite of the fact that a steamer pump was sent out from Poughkeepsie on a railroad flatcar. Panic reigned. Mattresses were carried downstairs and china was thrown out the window. The people of the hamlet came forward with offers to help rebuild, but Mr. Armstrong graciously refused and rebuilt the inn himself.

In 1871, the railroads were flourishing and with the station at the back of the inn, business at the inn expanded.

Mrs. Armstrong, H. G. Seaman, was a member of the Presbyterian Church across the street and when she came home from a ladies meeting and reported that objections had been voiced about the selling of liquor at the inn, Mr. Armstrong closed the bar and from then on the "best drink in the house" was water.

Mr. Armstrong died Aug. 27, 1919 and is buried in the Pleasant Valley Cemetery—a true "local".

According to the Town Clerk's records of the late 1800s, the Inn was frequently used as the meeting place for the Town Board.

From 1898 until 1926 there were five other owners and the inn had two name changes; Maple Shade and Grove Hall. But little history of the time span remains to report except for one typical "bar story" told by Claytonn Sands Doty who had a coal office in the inn during Hoctor's time.

According to Mr. Doty, one day a salesman was sounding forth at the bar and a local wit called him on the tale he was telling.

The salesman said, "Are you calling me a liar?.'

The "local" drawled, "No, but you sure sound just like I do when I lie."

When Walter Barth bought the property, the country was NOT enjoying prohibition and Walter spent the years from 1926-1933 serving meals and renting rooms As he waited for prohibition to be repealed, he did the interior walls with slab wood. He added old farm implements and household items as his decorations. At first he purchased the slabs from Bob Keller's sawmill and later from Don Robison who ran the mill behind the inn. Mr. Robison said that Mr. Barth insisted that the wood be cut in mid-winter because when cut then, it was less likely that the bark would loosen and fall off. The total effect had charm and the good food and service brought fame.

The Barths had a New Year's Party, patronized by the locals, each year and a good time was had by all.

Mr. and Mrs. Barth were very hard workers.For a while they had the New York Times delivered daily, They never had time to do more than scan it. They saw that the only one who was reading it from cover to cover was a neighbor who came in and ordered a cup of coffee for the reading. They canceled the subscription and when the neighbor realized the paper would not be forthcoming he discontinued his daily visit.

Mr. Barth's electrical power was on maximum power rate. He figured out that if he toasted a slice of bread in the electric toaster, once the lights went on at night, it cost him a phenominal amount of money. So at night if he had an order for toast he toasted it over the fire in the wood cook stove.

Another bar story! There were three cronies who would come in for a drink and one night they complained that they could get a bigger drink at Mike Bogles on upper Main Street in Poughkeepsie for less money. Later, another man came in and Walter asked him if he would go to Mike's bar, buy three shot glasses and bring them to him. Walt gave him some money and the man did as requested. The next time the cronies came in, Walter put three of HIS shot glasses on the bar and filled them, as requested. He then took Mike's glasses from beneath the bar and told the crones that these were in fact from Mike's and he poured from his shot glass into Mike's and each time he poured what was left in his glass, after filling Mike's, into the slop pail with a flourish.

Then he announced, "Here's your drink, gentlemen."

Clifford Buck made an effort to discover what happened to the acreage missing from sales since 1812. There are three pieces listed—all small, sold by Armstrong with the stipulation that there was to be no saloon and no gambling on the properties sold.

Clifford also found that Michael Hoctor sold two acres to the Pleasant Valley Elgin Creamery Co. This seems to be the old cider mill on West Road that was torn down to make way for Saw Mill Plaza.

When the railroad came into Pleasant Valley, the station was behind the inn. A right of way was granted between the department store and the inn. The land was to revert back to the inn property in the event the railroad became defunct. When this did happen in 1937, Irving Bower and Miles Carroll had an established coal business on the location. This happened during Walter Barth's proprietorship and he wanted the road closed, but Bower and Carroll won the lawsuit on the grounds that an established busineess could not be denied passage rignts.

James and Mabel Talbot were next in line. They too, had a long tenure and also were strong on community. Mrs. Talbot hosted the Library Fair on the side lawn of the inn for a number of years. The great success of the inn was the product of their fine hosting abilities. Before coming to Pleasant Valley they had a very popular restaurant on lower Main Street in Poughkeepsie called the "Fishnet." It was they who made the next big change to the exterior and interior of the inn. Part of the porch across the front was removed and a contemporary bay window was added. Inside, the bar was moved to this new area and the side wall alongside North Avenue was extended and a banquet room added.

The son of the Talbots, Michael, inherited the inn from his parents and ran it for awhile and then it was rented to Harry Maronas. He and his wife were the first to name the inn the "1830 Inn." They carried out the theme by dressing their waitresses in colonial costume.

The Inn burned again in July of 1981. Ronald Gasparro, a local developer, stepped in with plans to renovate the inn which he announced was still basically sound. He had plans to add a shopping plaza to the site. It took a year for approval and renovation and this delay canceled out the grandfather clause which would have allowed continuation of the original liquor permit. This caused a problem when the last proprietor applied. The new state law required that there be 200 feet from the front entrance of a church, synagogue or school to the entrance of the bar. In order to open the inn a new entrance had to be constructed at the back. Eileen Cudney and her associates had done a splendid job of redecorating. The delay, added expense and back entrance spelled doom. The 1830 Steak House opened December 30, 1984 and closed the following June. The place was emptied overnight leaving wedding reservations unfulfilled without explanations.

Plans for Mile Stone Square were approved in March 1989 and by March 15, 1990 those who mourned the Inn's fate stood watching the wrecking bar desecrate a grand old monument of the past that had stood and served as a landmark for 106 years.

Chronology

1826-1830	George W. Wood
1830-1865	Henry Flagler - 1830
	Zachariah S. Flagler - 1835
	Stephen Flagler - 1842
1865-1898	W. C. Armstrong
	burned and rebuilt in 1884
1898-1912	Michael Hoctor
1912-1913	Leonard Carpenter (Maple Shade)
1913- 1919	Charles and Grace Myers
1919-March-May	John E. & Edith A. Olmstead
	(Grove Hall)
1919-1924	Annie Grindle
1924-1926	Huga A. Olonson
1926-1951	Walter F. & Anne E. Barth
1951-1980	James & Mabel W. Talbot
1980-	Michael Talbot & Ann Cameron
	Harry Maronus (Rented-1830 Inn)
	Eileen Cudney (Rented-1830 Steak House)
1990- March 15th	Building Destroyed.

Remembering the 1830 Inn by Olive Doty was published by the town of Pleasant Valley Historical Society © February 1997.
GBG, Publishing, book design by George B. Greenwood 1997

The American Legion and Veterans Memorial

On December 10, 1919, Pleasant Valley American Legion Post #739 was organized by Charter Members: Charles H. Gillette, 1st Commander; D. Howard Bower, Dayton Burhans, Harry R. Cady; Louis W. Cady; Wesley I. Drake; Wm. J. Ehrlinger; Phillip F. Eichner; Herbert Lawrence, Charles W. Lovelace, Harold J. Mosher, Otto Ruehle, Jr., John F. Stevenson, John P. VanWagner and Harold W. Wilbur.

Not having a Post Home, the monthly meetings were at the homes of members. In 1934, the Legion purchased a Legion Home, which was a condemned school house on the Salt Point Road. In 1948, they sold the Legion Hall on Salt Point Road and purchased a lot on Route 44, east of Pleasant Valley, from Mrs. Edgar Peters, and proceeded to build a new Legion Home. This was completed and dedicated in 1950.

The American Legion provides Color Guards for local parades, they put flags on graves of all the veterans who are buried in various cemeteries around Pleasant Valley. They also collect worn and dirty flags to be burned in a ceremony.

Dedication of WW II Memorial, May 30, 1949 – Taken by Don Covert, Marten Berry was chairmen of the event.

Veteran's Memorial with the mill in the background. 1960's.

Veteran's Memorial showing Martin Berry's lilac hedge. At this time a second smaller plaque had been added for the names of more veterans.

Veteran's Memorial Route 44 and South Avenue before the corner was widened in winter.

During 2001 when Route 44 was widened this area was taken to widen the road. The three monument stones with plaques were taken to the American Legion Post #739 home on Route 44.

June of 2004 a new Veteran's Monument was dedicated, with a new design at the Mill Park Site. That monument contains names of members of the men and women who served in the Armed Services in many conflicts. It contains the names of 40 men who served during World War I, 210 men and women who served during World War II, 32 men who served during the Korean conflict, 62 men who served during the Vietnam conflict, 2 men who served during the Panama conflict, 3 men who served during Lebanon/Grenada, and 8 women and men who served during Desert Storm.

Imbedded in the lower level walkway are bricks, purchased by the public to honor individual Veterans for their service. Behind the Monument Stones are three flag poles on which fly the American flag with a POW/MIA flag in the center, the Pleasant Valley flag on the left and New York State flag on the right.

View of Monument at the Mill Site Park. circa 2009 (TeddiS)

The plaque, circa 2012 (PH)

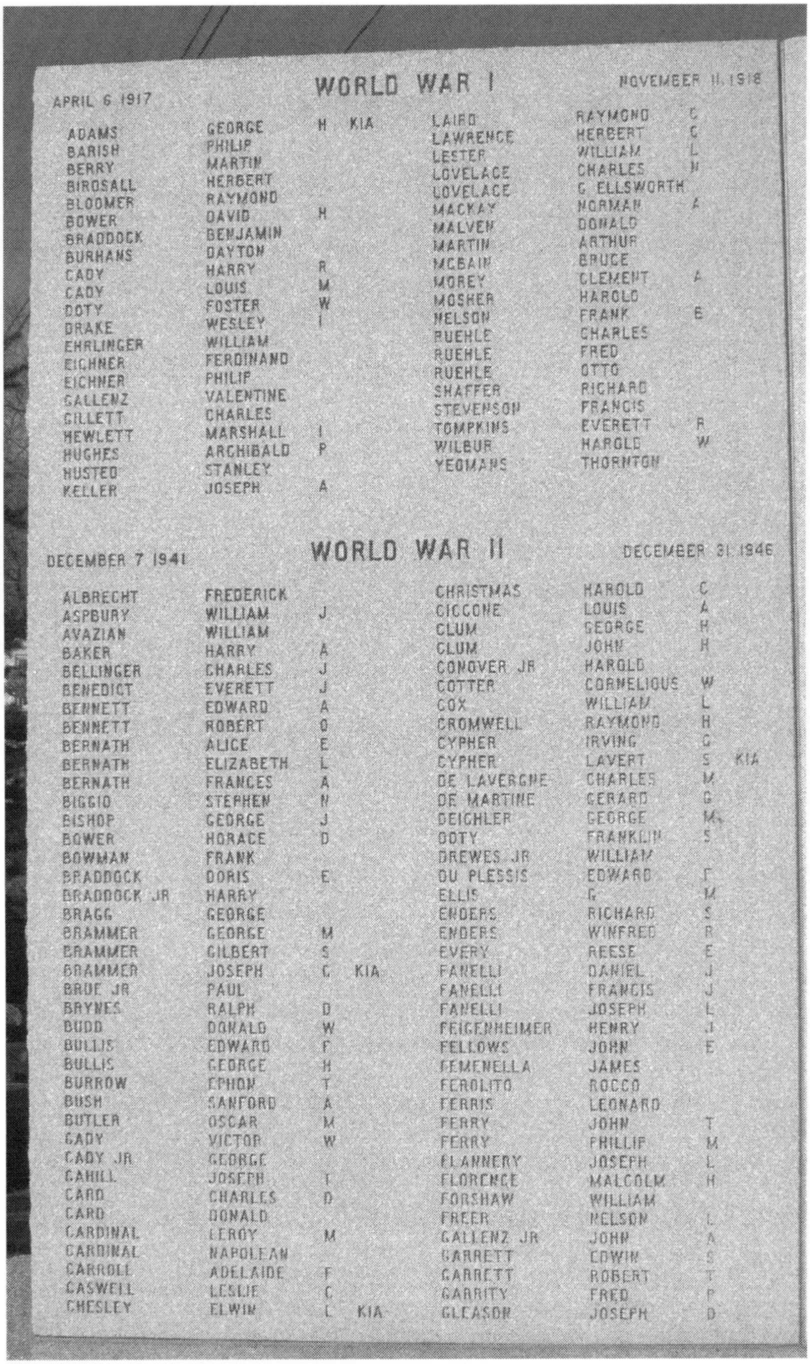

APRIL 6 1917 **WORLD WAR I** NOVEMBER 11 1918

ADAMS	GEORGE	H	KIA	LAIRD	RAYMOND	C
BARISH	PHILIP			LAWRENCE	HERBERT	C
BERRY	MARTIN			LESTER	WILLIAM	L
BIRDSALL	HERBERT			LOVELACE	CHARLES	H
BLOOMER	RAYMOND			LOVELACE	G ELLSWORTH	
BOWER	DAVID	H		MACKAY	NORMAN	A
BRADDOCK	BENJAMIN			MALVEN	DONALD	
BURHANS	DAYTON			MARTIN	ARTHUR	
CADY	HARRY	R		MCBAIN	BRUCE	
CADY	LOUIS	M		MOREY	CLEMENT	A
DOTY	FOSTER	W		MOSHER	HAROLD	
DRAKE	WESLEY	I		NELSON	FRANK	E
EHRLINGER	WILLIAM			RUEHLE	CHARLES	
EICHNER	FERDINAND			RUEHLE	FRED	
EICHNER	PHILIP			RUEHLE	OTTO	
GALLENZ	VALENTINE			SHAFFER	RICHARD	
GILLETT	CHARLES			STEVENSON	FRANCIS	
HEWLETT	MARSHALL	I		TOMPKINS	EVERETT	R
HUGHES	ARCHIBALD	P		WILBUR	HAROLD	W
HUSTED	STANLEY			YEOMANS	THORNTON	
KELLER	JOSEPH	A				

DECEMBER 7 1941 **WORLD WAR II** DECEMBER 31 1946

ALBRECHT	FREDERICK			CHRISTMAS	HAROLD	C	
ASPBURY	WILLIAM	J		CICCONE	LOUIS	A	
AVAZIAN	WILLIAM			CLUM	GEORGE	H	
BAKER	HARRY	A		CLUM	JOHN	H	
BELLINGER	CHARLES	J		CONOVER JR	HAROLD		
BENEDICT	EVERETT	J		COTTER	CORNELIOUS	W	
BENNETT	EDWARD	A		COX	WILLIAM	L	
BENNETT	ROBERT	O		CROMWELL	RAYMOND	H	
BERNATH	ALICE	E		CYPHER	IRVING	G	
BERNATH	ELIZABETH	L		CYPHER	LAVERT	S	KIA
BERNATH	FRANCES	A		DE LAVERGNE	CHARLES	M	
BIGGIO	STEPHEN	N		DE MARTINE	GERARD	G	
BISHOP	GEORGE	J		DEICHLER	GEORGE	M	
BOWER	HORACE	D		DOTY	FRANKLIN	S	
BOWMAN	FRANK			DREWES JR	WILLIAM		
BRADDOCK	DORIS	E		DU PLESSIS	EDWARD	F	
BRADDOCK JR	HARRY			ELLIS	G	M	
BRAGG	GEORGE			ENDERS	RICHARD	S	
BRAMMER	GEORGE	M		ENDERS	WINFRED	R	
BRAMMER	GILBERT	S		EVERY	REESE	E	
BRAMMER	JOSEPH	C	KIA	FANELLI	DANIEL	J	
BRUE JR	PAUL			FANELLI	FRANCIS	J	
BRYNES	RALPH	D		FANELLI	JOSEPH	L	
BUDD	DONALD	W		FEIGENHEIMER	HENRY	J	
BULLIS	EDWARD	F		FELLOWS	JOHN	E	
BULLIS	GEORGE	H		FEMENELLA	JAMES		
BURROW	EPHON	T		FEROLITO	ROCCO		
BUSH	SANFORD	A		FERRIS	LEONARD		
BUTLER	OSCAR	M		FERRY	JOHN	T	
CADY	VICTOR	W		FERRY	PHILLIP	M	
CADY JR	GEORGE			FLANNERY	JOSEPH	L	
CAHILL	JOSEPH	T		FLORENCE	MALCOLM	H	
CARD	CHARLES	D		FORSHAW	WILLIAM		
CARD	DONALD			FREER	NELSON	L	
CARDINAL	LEROY	M		GALLENZ JR	JOHN	A	
CARDINAL	NAPOLEAN			GARRETT	EDWIN	S	
CARROLL	ADELAIDE	F		GARRETT	ROBERT	T	
CASWELL	LESLIE	C		GARRITY	FRED	P	
CHESLEY	ELWIN	L	KIA	GLEASON	JOSEPH	D	

The left panel contains names from World War I and World War II.
circa 2012 (PH)

GOOD	EDWARD	T		OAKLEY	HERBERT		
GRAMMAS	JOHN			O HALLORAN JR	JOSEPH		KIA
GREEN	ROBERT			OLLIVETT	MARJORIE		
HAIGHT	DOUGLAS	D		OLLIVETT	WARREN	L	
HANCOCK	NELSON	E		OSTRANDER JR	HARRY		
HANCOCK	PERCY			PARKS	HARRY	B	
HANDLER	IRVING			PARKS	IRVING	C	
HARRINGTON	ROBERT	F		PARKS	RICHARD	M	
HASBROUCK	ALFRED			PETERS	EDGER	N	KIA
HASKINS JR	GUY	H		PHILIPBAR	JOHN		
HEVENOR	ROBERT	B		PHILIPBAR	THEODORE		
HEWLETT	ROBERT	W		PINK	ANDREW		
HOLST	RICHARD	P		PRYOR JR	RALPH		
HOWE	ALEXANDER	H		PULTZ	CHARLES	R	
HOWE	JOHN	C		PULTZ	CUSTER	H	
HUSTED	ALBERT	N		PURDY	ANNA	C	
IRELAND	CLARENCE	J		ROBERTS	JOSEPH	J	
IRELAND JR	JAMES			ROBINSON	STANLEY		
ISAKSEN	CARL			ROCHE	MAURICE		
JONES	VINCENT	P	KIA	ROE	HAROLD	G	
JUCHEM	FRANK			ROE	RALPH	E	
KARA	EDWARD			ROE JR	ARTHUR	F	
KELLER	LEONARD			ROGERS	CHARLES	A	
KEPFORD	JAMES	R		ROGERS	JAMES	H	
KIBBEE	HARRY	M		SAGENDORPH	HAROLD	L	
KILLMER	GEORGE	D		SALA	JOSEPH		
KIMLIN	JOHN	C		SANDERS	NOVEL	B	KIA
KING	JOHN	F		SCHERMERHORN	WILLIAM	E	
KROM JR	ROSCOE	W		SCHMIDT	HENRY		
LANE	IRVING			SCHMIDT	RUSSELL		KIA
LEIBE	ERNEST	G		SCOTT	KENNETH	L	
LEIBE	VIRGINIA	E		SEPE	WILLIAM		
LOVELACE	CLIFFORD	A		SHATTUCK	ALBERT		
LUZZI	JOSEPH	T		SHEA	DANIEL	J	
MACKEY	BERKLEY	C		SHELENBERG	WILLIAM		
MANN JR	JOHN	W		SHERMAN	FRANK	J	
MARSHALL	HOWARD	D		SHEROW	ALLEN	V	
MCALLISTER	ALEXANDER			SILVERNAIL	CHARLES	J	
MCALLISTER	FREDERICK			SILVERNAIL	EDWARD	F	
MCALLISTER	GEORGE			SILVERNAIL	STANLEY	A	
MCALLISTER	JOHN			SILVERNAIL	WILLIAM	R	
MCALLISTER	JOSEPH			SILVERNAIL JR	JOSEPH		
MCALLISTER	ROBERT			SMITH	ALBERT		
MCCABE	CHARLES			SMITH	RICHARD	A	
MCCARTHY	EDWARD	F		SOMMER	ROBERT	I	
MCCARTY	CHARLES	F		STOUTENBURGH	FRANK	J	
MCCLAY	JACK	S		STYLES	ROBERT	J	
MCCULLOCH	JOHN			STUPFER III	FRED		
MCCULLOUGH JR	EDWIN	B		SWARTZ	JAMES		
MCDONALD	CHARLES			SWARTZ	SAMUEL		
MCGRATH	ALFRED			SWEENEY	JAMES		
MEDDAUGH	GEORGE	E		SWEENEY	THOMAS		
MELVILLE	JOHN			TANNEN	SAMUEL	R	
MILLARD	FRANK	R		TEAL	DONALD	W	
MILLARD	JAMES	H		TEAL	PAUL	H	
MILLS	EDWARD	A		TERHUNE	BURTON	W	
MITTISKIE	ANTHONY			TICE	HARRISON		
MITTISKIE	EDWARD			TOMPKINS	CHARLES		
MITTISKIE	JOSEPH			TOMPKINS	LEWIS	D	
MITTISKIE	WILLIAM		KIA	TOOKER	HARRY		
MONTROSS	GEORGE	F		TOOKER	LEONARD		
MONTROSS	JOHN	T		TRAVER	ALDEN	R	
MONTROSS	KENNETH	R		VAN BUSKIRK	VINCENT		
MOREY	EARL			VAN VLACK	EARL	D	
MORTON	ROOSEVELT			VAN VOORHIS	RALPH	B	
NAUTA	BERT			VAN VOORHIS	RICHARD	E	
NAUTA	HARRY			VAN WAGNER	WILLIAM	D	

The next panel continues World War II.
circa 2012 (PH)

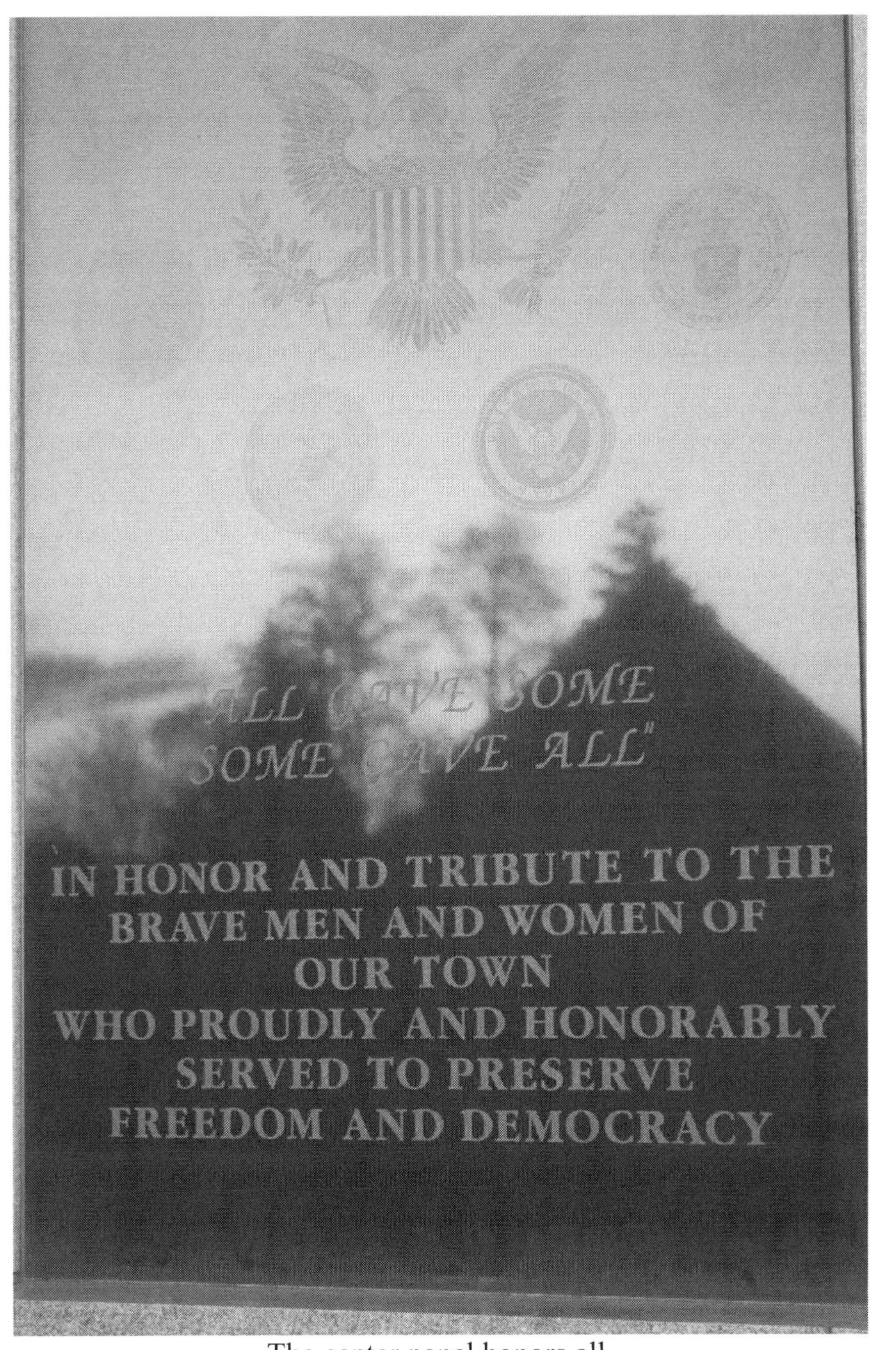

The center panel honors all.
circa 2012 (PH)

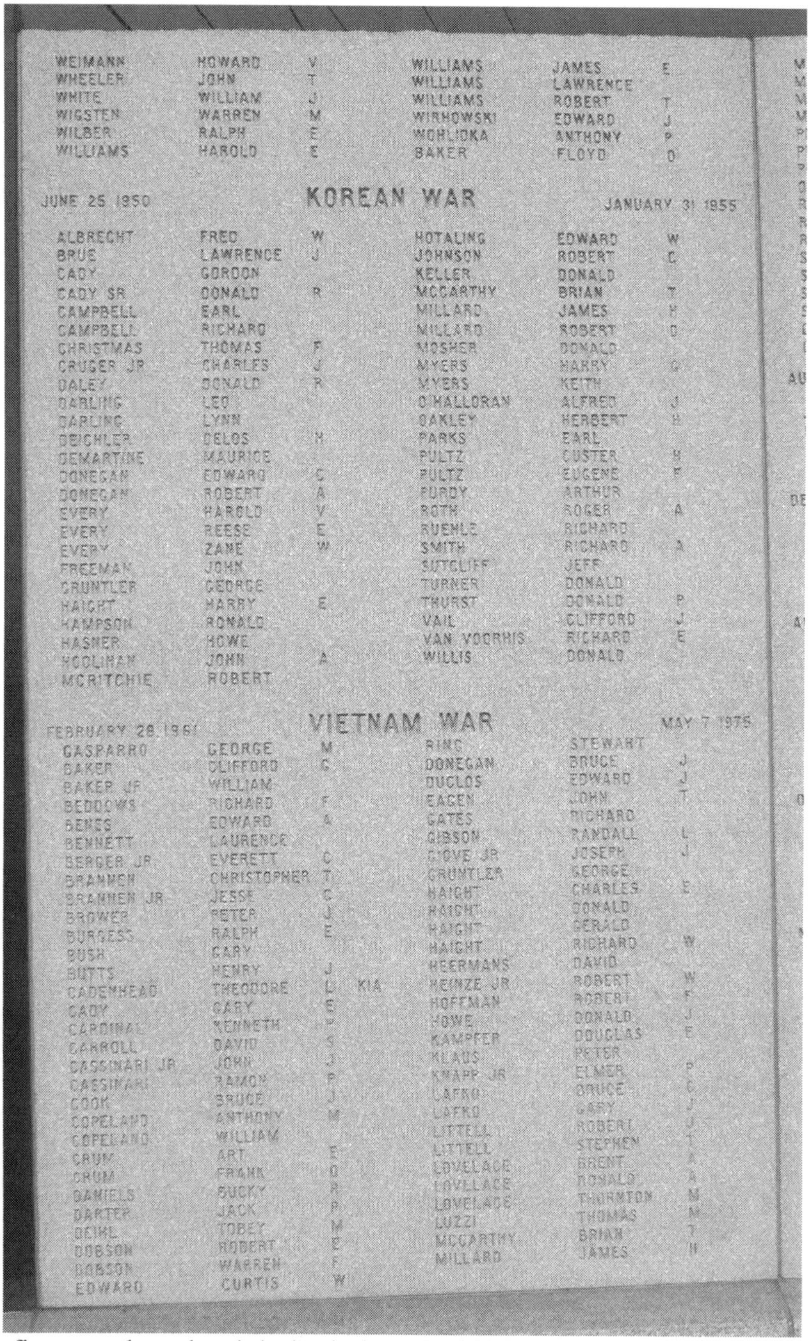

The first panel on the right includes World War II, the Korean War, and Vietnam War.
circa 2012 (PH)

The second panel on the right includes the Vietnam War, Lebanon/Grenada, Operation Just Cause-Panama, Operation Desert Shield/Storm, Operation Enduring Freedom Afghanistan, and Operation Iraqi Freedom. circa 2012 (PH)

Operation Skywatch

In front of the Skywatch building at what is now the intersection of West Road and Whiteford Drive, Martin Berry, Sara Nye, Virginia Berry, and Irma McCoy watch for planes and call to report sightings. Picture taken 1953.

"In early 1950, the Continental Air Command formed a 8,000 post civilian Ground Observer Corps to supplement what would become the North American Aerospace Defense Command (NORAD). Over 200,000 volunteers participated in nationwide drills, telephoning dozens of coordination centers which in turn relayed information to the Air Defense Command (ADC) ground control interception centers.

By 1952 the program was expanded with a new organizational plan named Operation Skywatch with over three-quarters of a million volunteers taking shifts at over 16 thousand posts and 75 relay centers.

> By the late 1950s, a major semi-automatic aircraft warning and detection system had been developed, Semi Automatic Ground Environment (SAGE), and was in the early stages of installation. Due to the dramatic technological improvements provided by this new system, the Air Force cancelled the Ground Observer Corps program in 1959."[w]

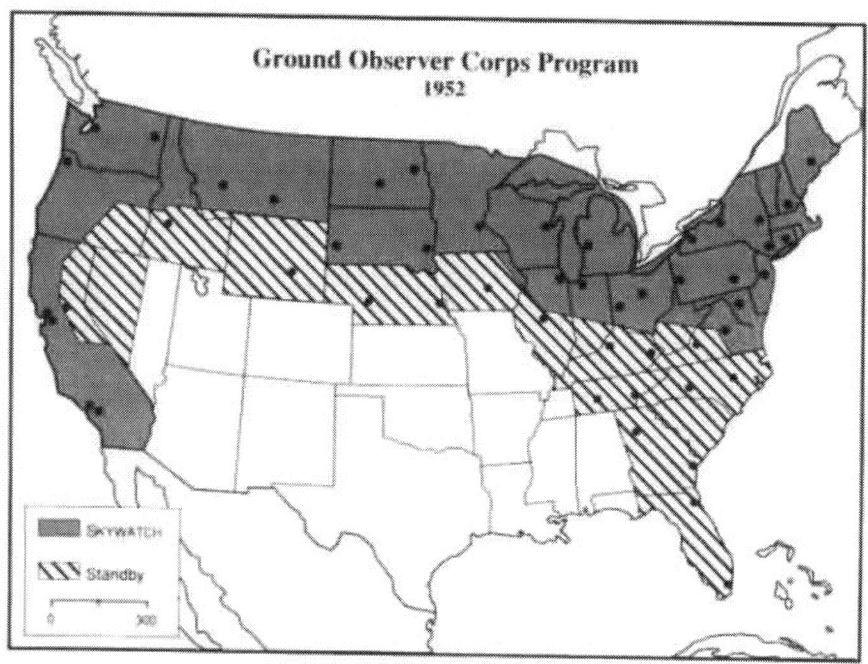

http://radomes.org/museum/documents/GOC/GOC.html

"What were they watching for?

Looking back, the idea of a bomber hitting the US from Europe or Asia in the 1950s seems implausible, but this was a time when it seemed prudent to expect the worst.

It was the era when the Soviets acquired nuclear weapons. Like us, the Soviets had captured German scientists and had them working on intercontinental delivery systems. And who knew what kind of long-range aircraft the USSR had in operation?

There was also Red China, about which we knew even less. By the end of June 1950, we were at war in Korea, and, not long after that, Mao Zedong's China plunged into the war on the side of North Korea.

The US government and public took the threat seriously. Many built bomb shelters. Others stocked up on canned goods and checked out which local buildings were designated as public shelters. School children practiced the 'duck and cover' technique and were warned to stay away from windows during an attack."[x]

An article in the Poughkeepsie Journal of February 12, 1950, headlined:

"Valley Aircraft Warning Service Organized, Martin Berry To Head Group" states that Pleasant Valley Supervisor Cecil Sherow appointed Martin Berry as supervisor of the Pleasant Valley post of the Dutchess County Aircraft Warning Service. Homer Teal was named assistant supervisor. Citizens of the community who consented to serve in setting up a permanent organization for national defense locally are Haig Babian, Mr. and Mrs. Darius Benson, Mr. and Mrs. Clarence Bernholz, Mr. and Mrs. Lewis Bicknell, Mrs. John Campbell, Donald Covert, Mr. and Mrs. William Dederer, Edward Hughes, William LaBarge, Mr. and Mrs. Edward Markowski, Mr. and Mrs. Erven Meddaugh, Edward McCarthy, Mrs. Daniel McDonald, Mrs. Bert Adam, Mr. and Mrs. Glenn Myers, Mr. an Mrs. Kenneth Sherow, Mr. and Mrs. Robert Smith, John Stewart, Burton Stickles, Paul Teal, Archer Woodwell. Leland H. Shaw Jr., of Poughkeepsie, was general chairman of the Dutchess County Aircraft Warning Service.

An article in the Poughkeepsie Journal, Sunday, April 15, 1951, page 3 reported that more than 100 volunteers of the town of Pleasant Valley attended a meeting of the Ground Observers' corps at the American Legion home on Monday night April 9, 1951.

An article in the Poughkeepsie Journal, August 10, 1952 reported that during August 1952 a new lookout building was built and being used for the observers on West Road. The upper half of the building was made of glass ventilating windows on all sides. It was built with one side due north, set by compass, the post has compass direction fins both inside and outside. The modern observation building, is shown in the picture on the following page with Mr. and Mrs. Johnson. For the previous 3 years the post was located at the American Legion home east of the village. The construction of the new site began July 28, 1952 by Assistant Chief Observer Clarence Bernholz, John B. Huntley and Martin Berry, Post supervisor. Ground observers started operations in the new building at 6 p.m. on August 1, 1952.

Mr. and Mrs. H. Maynard Johnson of Pleasant Valley took their turn watching for planes in December, 1952.

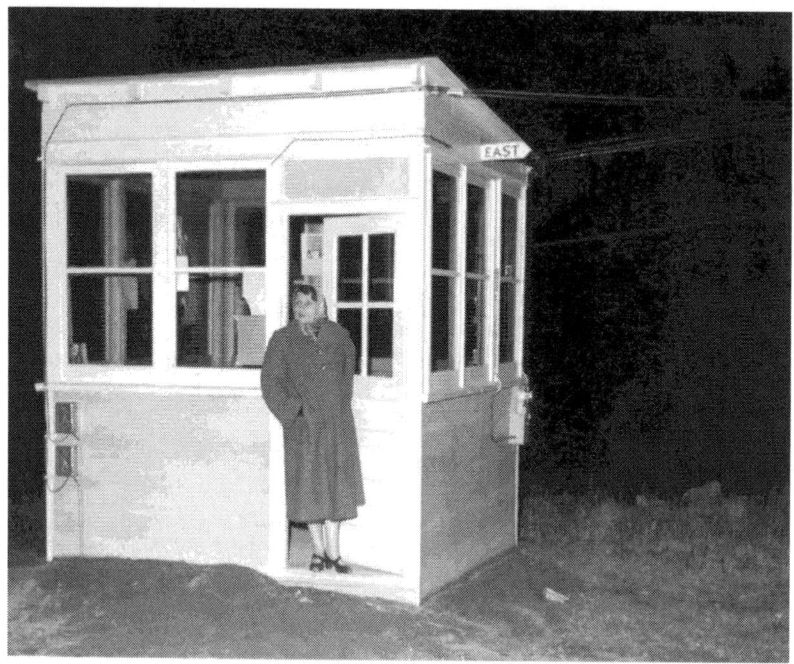

Mrs. Johnson standing outside the observation station on West Road.

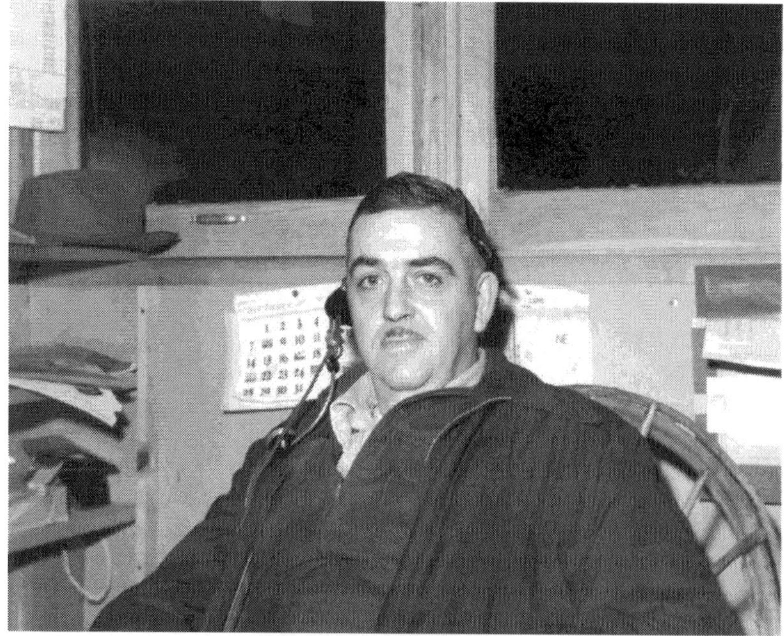

Mr. H. Maynard Johnson inside the observation station.

When the Ground Observer Corps was inactivated each volunteer recieved a letter signed by Dwight D. Eisenhower, the President of he United States at the time, that read as follows:

"TO EACH GROUND OBSERVER CORPS VOLUNTEER:

The inactiation of the Ground Observer Corps on January 1, 1959, will terminate the longest continuous service in peacetime by civilian volunteers engaged in support of our national defense effort. I commend you for heeding the call to voluntary service in providing a strong air defense against any would-be invader of our skies and for your loyal devotion to the cause of freedom. Our country is indebted to you for your steadfast, unselfish and willing service in a cause of vital importance to our air defense. I salute you on this occasion for a job well done and ask for a continuation of your devoted and patriotic service in meeting the challenges of the future.

I hope that you will continue to provide leadership in other fields of civil defense and by your example stimulate many other Americans to share in the task required to sustain our democratic way of life.

/s/ Dwight D. Eisenhower"

Carson Robison

Carson Robison is the man in the center, the five men around him are members of his band. (GBG)

If you were a teenager during the 1950's you might have learned to square dance to the music of Carson Robison at the school on Traver Road or you might have gone to the American Legion Hall on Friday night's to dance to his music.

Carson was an accomplished guitarist and a virtual virtuoso at whistling, in 1932 he started his own band, they continued touring and recording through the 1930's and 1940's. He recorded many records and albums. He also played at the Grand Ole Opry in the 1940's and 1950's, and his music can still be purchased from his website www.carsonrobison.com.

He was inducted into the western Music Association Hall of Fame in 2001.

People may remember Carson's son Don who ran the saw mill for years. Don and his wife Jean lived on the hill overlooking the Mile Stone Square Plaza at the corner of Main Street and North Avenue.

Carson Robison died 1957 at Poughkeepsie, New York.[y]

The Falcons Junior Marching Band

The Falcons Marching Band, Inc. was founded by Nick Pozza in July of 1975 and continued to please crowds for more than 10 years.

In September of 1975, under the musical direction of Mr. Jerry Conklin, the Falcons made their debut in Pleasant Valley, in the town's annual weekend celebration parade. The band's colors were lime green and white, designed by Nick. The uniforms were tailor made for each member.

The Falcons were an independent organization made up of people who donated their time and talents. Operating expenses were offset by donations, performance fees, and fund raising events', such as jewelry and fashion show at the Presbyterian Church in November 1977, and a special fund raiser at the Civic Center in 1984 to replace the group's 1964 equipment van. The new van was able to be on the road to take their equipment to the next show in Big Indian, New York later that year.

From 42 members in July of 1975 the band grew to 102 members in April 1984. The members of the band ranged in age from 10 to 21. All band members were able to read music, and the color guard members, who were between 14 and 18, learned complex routines. Parents of members volunteered to serve as "guide-ons" during engagements to walk with the marchers to provide help if needed. Every year they ended the season with a picnic at James Baird State Park in Freedom Plains.

The Falcons Marching Band played at many exciting events, including: Dutchess Community College for the Special Olympics, Lake Placid and Lake George; the German Alps Festival, West Point; Hofstra University as host for the Senior Drum Corps Competition, 3 pre-game shows at Yankee Stadium; and a pre-game and halftime show at Giant Stadium at the Meadowlands. The band also put in numerous appearances for the various fire companies, including some as far away as Sharon and Canaan, Connecticut, and has performed at the Dutchess County Fair, the State Elks Convention in Wildwood, New Jersey and Mayors Day Trophy Parade in Paramus, New Jersey, as well as a 300th anniversary celebration in Danbury, Connecticut.

The following poem sums up the feeling of the members of the band:

Pride in Being a Falcon

Win or lose, be proud of what you are…
Doing your best will take you far.
Beyond today and into tomorrow…
Thru happy days and times of sorrow.

Take pride in what <u>you</u> do,
And the best of each member will shine through.
We started as one man's dream…
And have become a marching team.

One hundred and two people to fit…
"This waist we'll take in just a bit."
Shiny shoes and boots of cleanest white…
No wonder the Falcon's are a welcome sight!

Shh! I hear them coming…
Listen…you can feel the drumming.
Here they are - - and what a fine band.
The songs that are played…and they look just grand.

All of the work and practice surely pays…
Just listen to those kids and how they play!
Color guard and flash flags lead you in,
To the winners circle again and again.

Lessons learned and responsibilities met,
Will aid you in your quest to get.
The most from life - - because you tried,
And this after all is a thing called pride.

By: Carolyn Fowler
2/20/79

The photographer and dates of the following photographs are unknown. The last photo was noted as being taken in 1978. All photographs shown here are properties of the Pleasant Valley Historical Society.

Pictures taken 1983 or 1984

Falcons 1978

Parade in Pleasant Valley, picture taken 1978

Parade in Pleasant Valley June 1978

Wildwood, New Jersey, picture taken June 7, 1986

Wildwood, New Jersey, picture taken June 7, 1986

Major Floods of Pleasant Valley

.

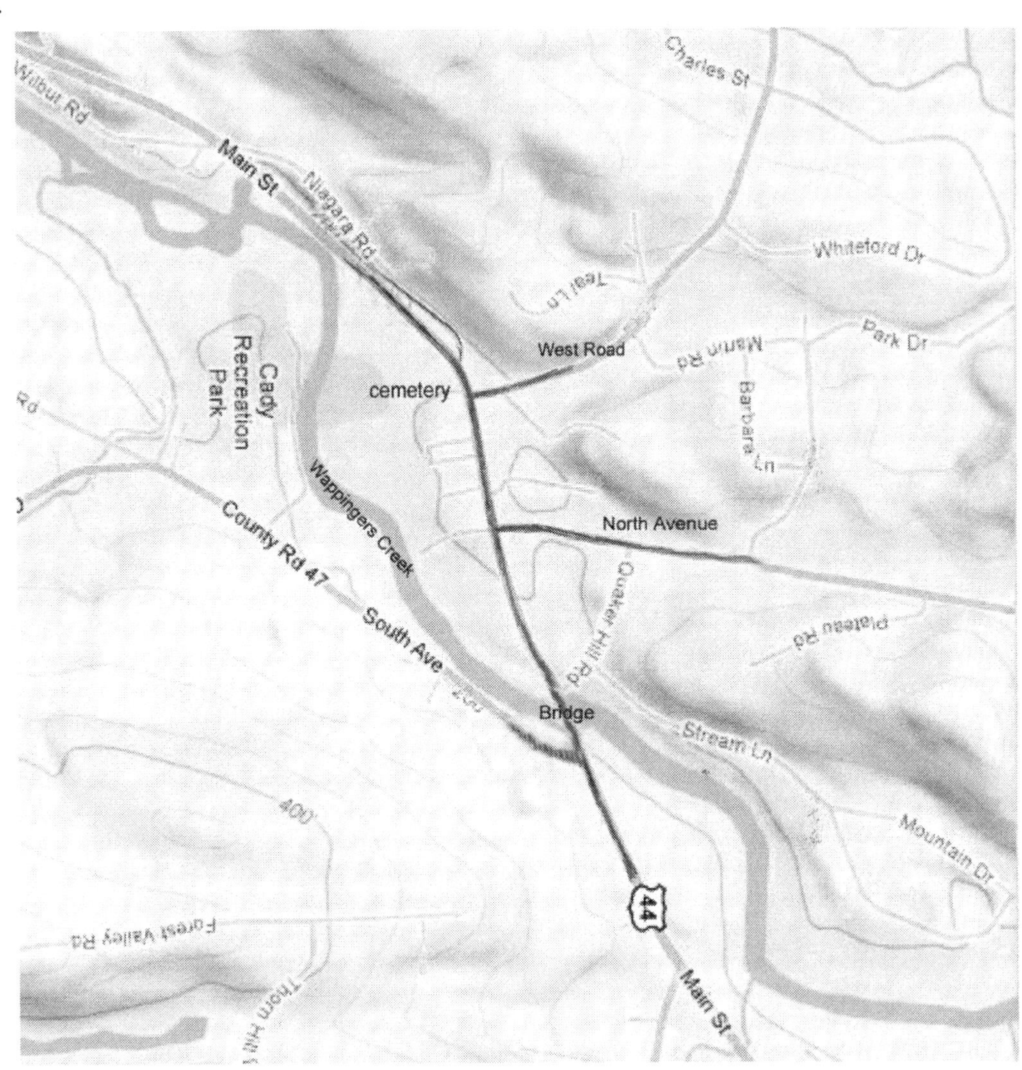

Flood of 1902

Although there are limited newspaper articles or other information about the flood of 1902, there were three pictures of a flood listed as 1902, among the other flood pictures in a folder, made by George Greenwood on the Historical Society computer.

Flood of 1902, North Avenue.(GBG)

Flood of 1902, Quaker Hill Road and Main Street.(GBG)

Flood of 1902, taken from South Avenue.(GBG)

Flood of 1938

September 1938, Pleasant Valley felt the effects of the wind and rain of what NOAA (National Oceanic and Atmospheric Administration) called "The Great New England Hurricane of 1938." (When hurricane naming practices began in 1953 hurricanes were named for women, prior to that they were named for the region affected.)

The combined effects from both the weather system and the hurricane produced rainfall of 10 to 17 inches, resulting in some of the worst floods ever recorded in this area.

The hurricane was also referred to by some sources as the "Long Island Express." According to NOAA, when it passed to the north of Puerto Rico on the 18th and 19th it was likely a category 5 hurricane. It turned northward on September 20th and by morning of the 21st it was 100 to 150 miles east of Cape Hatteras, North Carolina. At that point, the hurricane accelerated to a forward motion of 60 to 70 mph, making landfall over Long Island and Connecticut that afternoon as category 3. [z]

The Poughkeepsie Eagle News of September 22 & 23, 1938 reported the following information:

As the Wappingers Creek rose upstream from Pleasant Valley, two people, including a Pleasant Valley fireman, were drowned, in the raging waters near Lefty Atwater's Idlewild tavern on Creek Road. The restaurant, about one mile northeast of the hamlet of Pleasant Valley, was near a small camp ground on the shore of the Wappingers Creek.

At least four other people, including members of the rescue party, were reportedly found clinging to trees where they took refuge after being hurled into the water when their craft capsized. They had been in the trees from shortly before 10 o'clock the evening of September 21 to about 5 o'clock the following morning.

Kenneth Larkin, a 22 year old Pleasant Valley fireman and member of the first rescue party, rushed to a point opposite Lefty Atwater's tavern to take two women from a camp that was nearly submerged by water, and became one of the victims himself.

Dubois Haight, chief of the Pleasant Valley Fire Department, Chester Carlson, and William Millard set out in a small boat and took the two women in the boat. They started for land but the boat turned over. All five of them reached trees, Haight went back after those in the trees and took the two girls in the boat. The boat capsized and one of the girls was washed down the stream.

When the rescue boat overturned, Mrs. Keefe, 25, wife of Daniel J. Keefe, and neighbor of Mrs. Ferguson at Astoria, took refuge in a tree for more than eight hours before she was finally rescued by Fireman Ralph Beacham of Arlington. Larkin was clinging to a tree when he attempted to reach Mrs. Keefe, and plunged into the rushing waters.

William Millard, it was said, gripped a tree near the spot where the boat overturned and clung there until 4:30 A.M. when a life line was thrown to him and he was pulled to shore.

Displaying heroism in the battle to save those who had been hurled into the flood water, were Chester Carlson, DuBois Haight, chief to Pleasant Valley Fire Department; Ralph Beacham Arlington Fire Department; Arlington Fire Chief Ghee, and Kenneth Martin, Arlington paid driver.

Members of the rescue party headed by Fire Chief Arthur L. Ghee of Arlington praised the courage of Mrs. Keefe, who secured her arms to a tree with vines and remained calm for more than eight hours until she was rescued.

The two victims, recovered from the muddy waters just south of the Idlewild tavern were identified as Kenneth Larkin, 22, son of Mrs. Florence Larkin, a Pleasant Valley fireman and employee of the Pleasant Valley Finishing company; and Caroline Ferguson, 21 of 330 49th street, Astoria, Long Island, New York.

Picture of Kenneth Larkin, 22 year old Pleasant Valley Fireman and hero who drowned while attempting to rescue Ruth Keefe from the raging waters of the Wappingers Creek.

Photographer and date of picture unknown.

As the tragedy was taking place near Creek Road, downstream the hamlet water was rising and spilling over the banks of the creek above the bridge and dam. It flowed down Main Street into side streets and homes, washing out yards and railroad tracks.

West Road at the junction of Main Street. Masten's Feed Store on right, looking toward the Presbyterian Cemetery.(GBG)

A back yard on South Avenue and the mill, from east bank of Wappingers Creek.(GBG)

Note from Poughkeepsie Eagle News article: Fireman Beacham suffered from exposure yesterday morning and he went to Idlewild Tavern where he rested.

My note: During the years of prohibition Lefty Atwater's establishment, Idlewild Tavern, was a speakeasy.

During the early years of television I remember my parents taking me to the home of Lefty and Henrietta Atwater to watch TV on their small black and white TV with an almost round screen. The whole room was dark except for the glowing images. We watched I Love Lucy and Lights Out Theater.

Flood of 1955

In August of 1955 Hurricane Diane, following close on the heels of Hurricane Connie, brought rain, wind and flooding to Pleasant Valley.
According to NOAA (National Oceanic and Atmospheric Administration)[aa], Hurricane Connie produced generally 4 to 6 inches of rainfall on August 11 and 12. Hurricane Diane came a week later and the rainfall from Diane ranged up to nearly 20 inches over a two day period.
This was before the days of cell phones. Telephone company operators in Poughkeepsie said there would be a delay of one and one-half hours in placing calls to Pleasant Valley, according to the Poughkeepsie New Yorker, page one article on August 19, 1955. There was no way to get into or out of Pleasant Valley. According to Pleasant Valley Highway Superintendent Gleason, approximately 500 families were affected by the flood after a day's rain which doused the area with seven inches of water.
Also reported on August 19, 1955 in the Poughkeepsie New Yorker:

> "A three room house completely furnished was swept from its foundation along the south side of Dutchess Turnpike just south of Pleasant Valley. The home was owned by Mr. and Mrs. William Hawley, and was occupied by Mr. and Mrs. William Houston. Mr. Houston is a photographer.
> Mr. and Mrs. Houston evacuated their home during the night but 'When we left last night we didn't think it was so bad, so we didn't take anything but the clothes we wore.' Mrs. Houston said. 'We've lost everything.'
> The house was seen about a quarter mile from its original site still being carried along by the creek waters."

On the east edge of the hamlet where the town hall currently is, the water was said to be five to seven feet deep over the highway.
The paper further reported that the electric power had to be turned off to the town by Central Hudson Gas and Electric Corporation at 10:15 am.
Donald Robison, a rescue worker, was hauling stalled cars out of flooded areas when his tractor tipped over. He swam over to a nearby telephone pole which he climbed to await rescue.
According to the Highway superintendent, water in the village was between three and four feet high. It was up to the front of houses and stores and also

inside some of the buildings.

Tractors and highway trucks were used to evacuate residents trapped in their homes by the flood. One resident, a teenager at the time, remembers being taken in a dump truck from the center of the village to the Pleasant Valley School on Traver Road, where the Red Cross was to set up a shelter. She was worried because she had to leave her dog behind in her home. Later in the day the sun came out, she joined a friend to walk back to the village. They walked down Main Street where the water was knee high, not thinking about how contaminated the water might be. When she got to her home she found that her dog was fine.

According to the Poughkeepsie New Yorker August 20, 1955, Dr. Gordon C. MacKenzie, Town of Pleasant Valley health officer, warned residents whose homes were in the flooded area of the township, not to use water from their wells for drinking purposes; until he and the State Department of Health Inspectors tested the water. Tank trucks with water were stationed in front of the firehouse, the school, and the Grange hall.

A gas tank containing 1,800 pounds of bottled gas broke loose from the mill and was carried down the creek to Rochdale where it became wedged between two trees and a baseball backstop. (Almost 3 miles along the creek)

Reportedly eighteen caskets on show in the display room of the Allen funeral home in Main Street were ruined by the flood waters.

Several bottled gas and septic tanks snapped loose from buildings. Cows, horses and trees were seen being swept over the dam.

August 20, 1955 Poughkeepsie New Yorker reported:

> "Yesterday's floods were worse than the 1938 hurricane, according to Professor A. Scott Warthin, geologist at Vassar College and chairman of the Dutchess County Water Conservation committee.
>
> While the torrential waters in Wappingers Creek washed away the equipment of the U. S. Geological Survey station there. Professor Warthin estimated the peak flow at 17,000 cubic feet per second. That flow compared with a peak of 15,900 cubic feet per second reached during the 1938 hurricane. Yesterday's peak at Red Oaks Mill occurred at 3:30 p.m."

Highway superintendent Gleason said this flood was worse than 1938 in terms of the amount of water and damage, but this time it was better because the crest came at noon on a sunshiny day; at midnight with a 50 mile wind blowing.

As the lower portion of the Wappingers Creek backed up and overflowed its banks, the water covered portions of Route 44, and was moving through the cemetery, onto Main Street. In some of these pictures cars are still able to drive through the water.

H. Maynard Johnson lived near the Ford Garage, and took many pictures of the scene as the water became higher.

The water coming from the Wappingers Creek near the bridge flowing down Main Street joined with the water moving up Main Street, and the entire street including the houses and business in the village were flooded.

Local highway department employees, volunteers from the fire department, and citizens with big trucks or tractors braved the flood waters to rescue residents of Pleasant Valley.

Following are some pictures taken at various stages of the flood.

Town truck rescuing stranded residents. (HMJ)

Water flowing over the stone wall fence surrounding the cemetery.(HMJ)

The cemetery under water. (HMJ)

The G. E. Masten Feed Store view from the cemetery. (GBG)

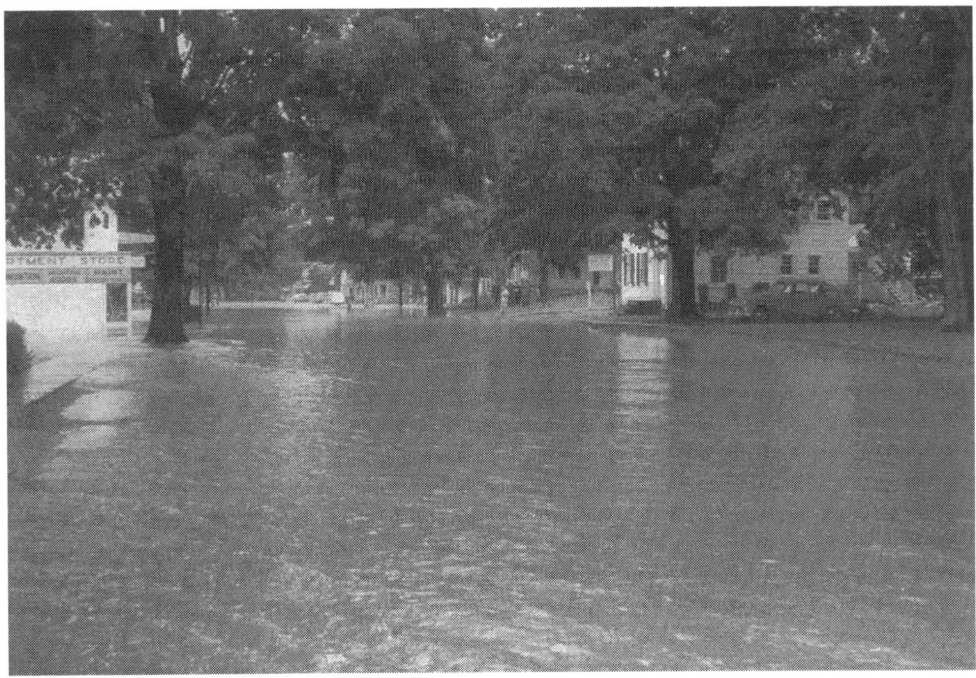

Main Street looking west, the Department Store is still there, on the left, the tree in front of it is gone.

Looking from North Avenue toward small strip mall along Main Street. This strip mall in this picture was torn down to make way for a small shopping center in about 1971. (HMJ)

South side of Main Street, looking from North Avenue across, toward the Pleasant Valley Hotel. This historic structure was razed to make way for a shopping mall.

The Mail must go through!

Post Master "Pat" Clark with Edna Hommel, Chub Parks, Dorcus Brower and Mary Parks carrying the mail out of the flooded Post Office.(EH)

Ed Smith driving the truck, Chub Parks and Post Master "Pat" Clark carrying boxes of mail, Edna Hommel on the truck.(EH)

The home of Archie Smith and his family, the house was behind the old firehouse, it is where the current driveway and parking lot for the current firehouse.

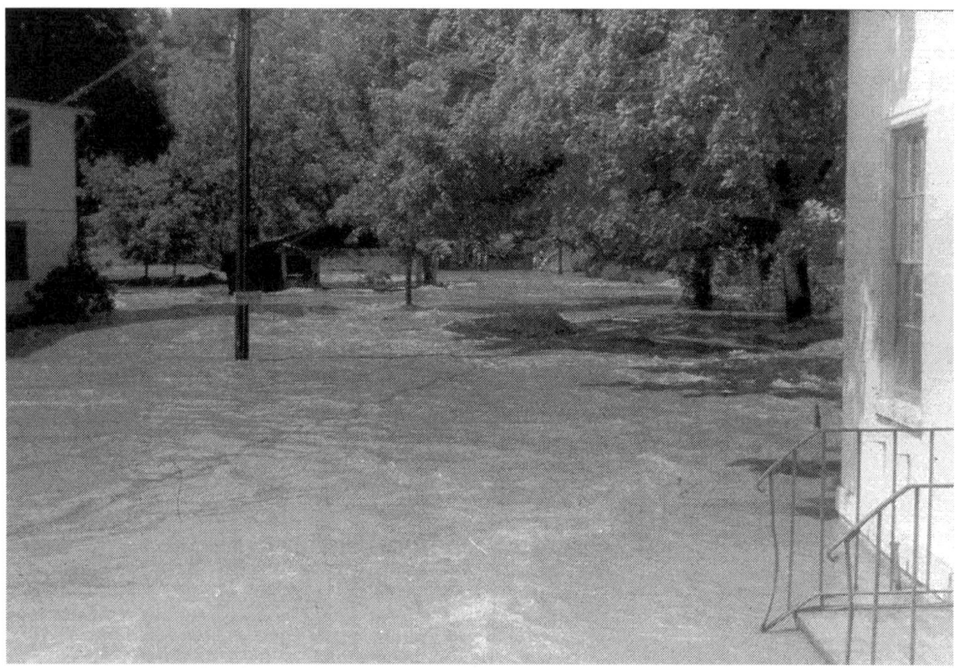

View looking down Quaker Hill Road from Main Street.

At one point the water was going in the back windows of this house and out the front. The house is the second house on the east side of Quaker Hill Road, near Main Street. The name of the family at the time was Brinckerhoff.

Looking from the bridge on Main Street into town.

One of the larger bridges in the county, a 100 foot long span that crossed Wappingers Creek on Hurley Road, near Salt Point was destroyed. (HMJ)

The skeleton of the bridge lying in the Wappingers Creek. This bridge survived the great flood of 1938. (HMJ)

Workmen of the Smith Construction Company, Pelham, New York, which had a $92,898 government flood control contract for Wappingers Creek at Pleasant Valley planned to lower the dam, build a larger retaining wall north of the Dutchess turnpike bridge, and do some channel straightening and deepening which eventually was designed to make water available for fire fighting. this became a cause for concern with the lowering of the water level.

Many people watched June 4, as a "Chunk" was taken from the dam to lower the water level of the Wappingers Creek. The depth of the water above the dam had been about nine or ten feet, after the lowering of the dam the depth would be two or three feet.

Now the Fire Department owns and maintains the old mill pump house that used to supply water for the sprinkler system in the mill. It is difficult to keep the pit clean enough to provide a good supply of water, since the water level is so low. The fire district also gets water from behind the plaza and the boat launch in Cady Recreation Park.[bb]

View of the creek after the dam was lowered.

Flood of 1973

The test of the dam lowering and the retaining wall came in July of 1973 when disaster struck. Severe storms and flooding, caused a major disaster to be declared July 20, 1973. [cc]

Although the creek still backed up on the west side of town and flooded the Cady Recreation Park and part of the Presbyterian cemetery, the water did not overflow the retaining wall near the bridge.

Looking at the parking lot and Mike Cady Recreation Center.

The Presbyterian cemetery in July 1973.

The bridge at Hurley Road that was destroyed in the 1955 flood and rebuilt.

Flood of 2007

Disaster in the form of flooding struck again in April, 2007. A state of emergency was declared in several Dutchess County towns, including Pleasant Valley.

Supervisor Jeff Battistoni declared a state of emergency from Tuesday, April 17 to 4 p. m. Friday, April 21. The town government was temporarily relocated to the town highway garage on Sherow road. [dd]

Residents of Shady Creek neighborhood were evacuated, and a temporary Red Cross shelter was available at Saint Stanislaus Church.

By April 18, the Poughkeepsie Journal reported that all roads were open in Pleasant Valley, but the town hall was closed due to flooding. Flood waters closed a stretch of Route 44 in front of the town hall, The building was closed after the water receded to clean up from the flooding.[ee]

The Town Hall as it looked April, 2007.(TerriG)

The Wappingers Creek, very close to the edge of the sidewalk at the Mill Site Park. (TerriG)

The Dam, taken from the Mill Site Park. (TerriG)

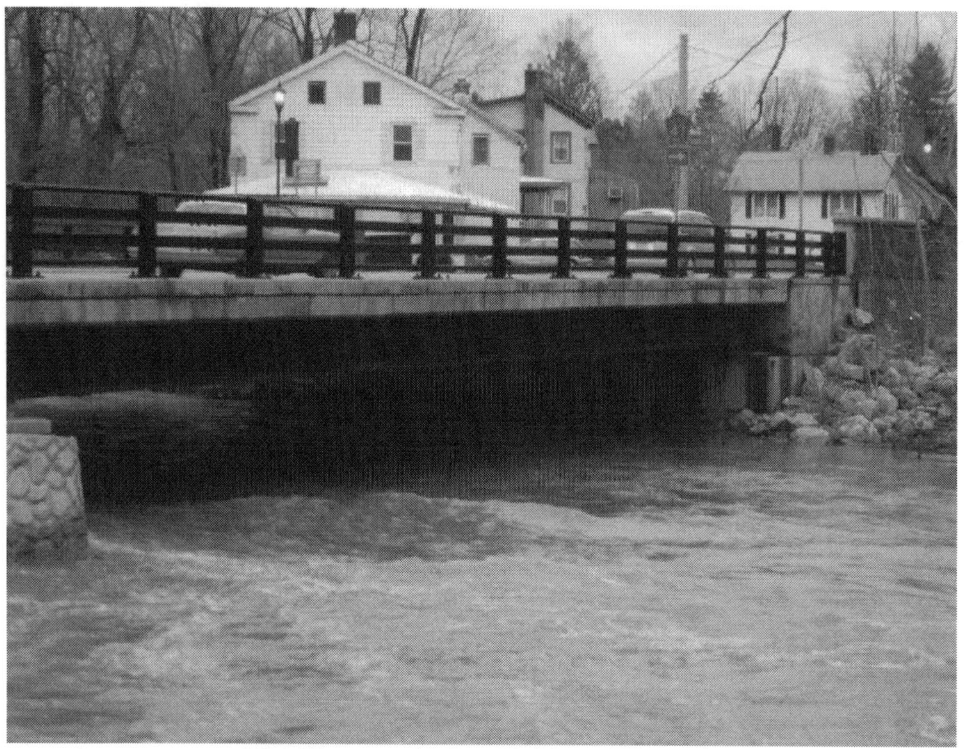

The Pleasant Valley Bridge. (JRoosa)

Water splashed up through the grates on the Hurley Road Bridge. (BShapley)

Flood of 2011

Once again Dutchess County prepared for a hurricane, and emergency operations centers were activated. As Hurricane Irene struck the northeast causing disaster in the form of flooding, on August 31, a state of emergency was declared in several Dutchess County towns, including Pleasant Valley.[ff] The Wappingers Creek overflowed its banks, flooding the Presbyterian Cemetery, Mike Cady Recreation Park, the Town Hall, and parts of Route 44.

The dam from the back of the Mill Site Park. (PVSuperv)

Mike Cady Recreation Park. (PVSuperv)

Town Hall parking lot with Mike Cady Recreation field. (BShapley)

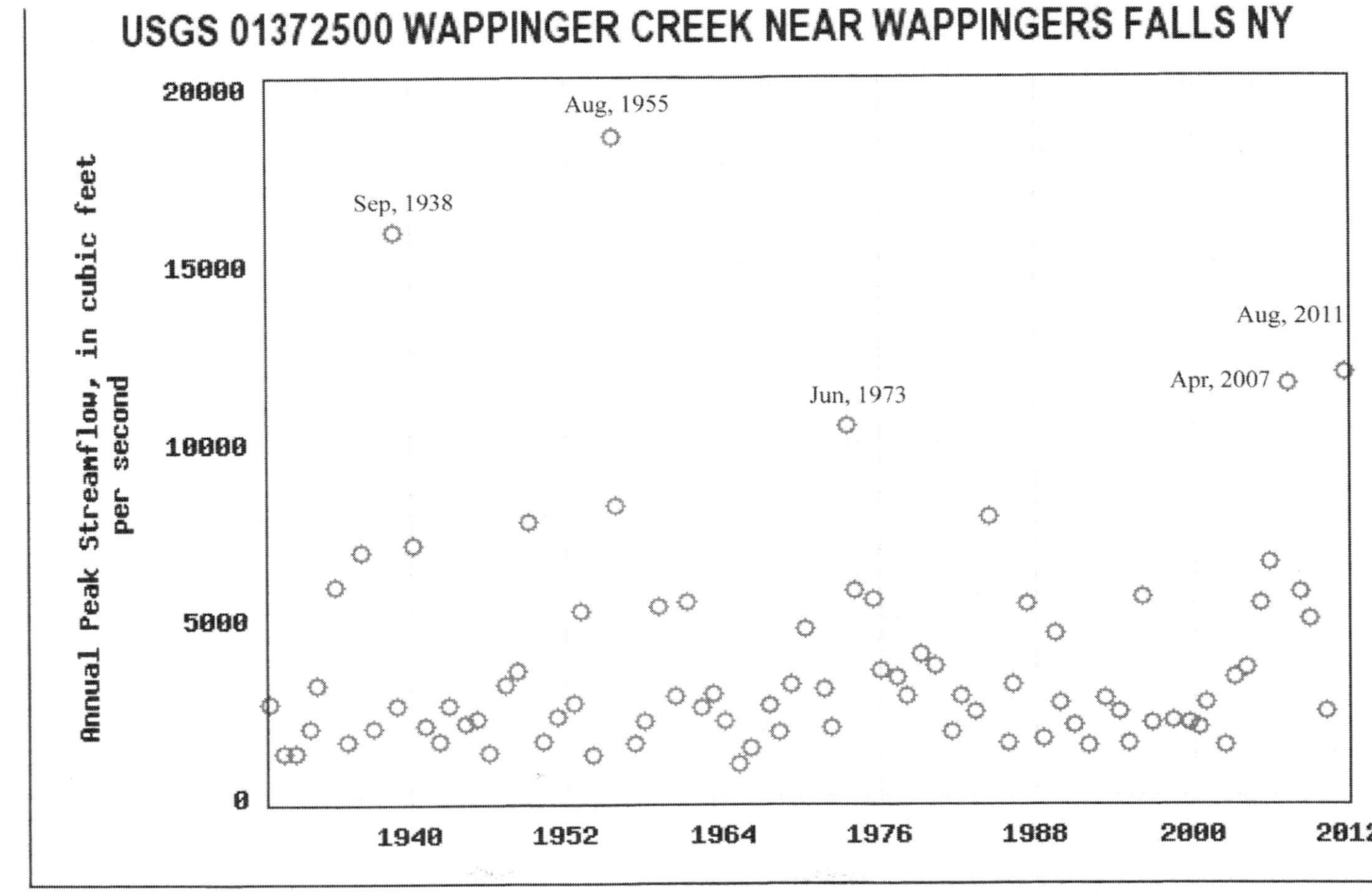
USGS 01372500 WAPPINGER CREEK NEAR WAPPINGERS FALLS NY
Annual Peak Streamflow, in cubic feet per second
20000
15000
10000
5000
0
1940
1952
1964
1976
1988
2000
2012
Aug, 1955
Sep, 1938
Aug, 2011
Apr, 2007
Jun, 1973
Surface Water for USA: Peak Streamflow
http://nwis.waterdata.usgs.gov/ny/nwis/peak?site_no=01372500&agency_cd=USGS&format=img

Pleasant Valley Department Store

The following information is copied from the website: http://pleasantvalleydepartmentstore.com/aboutus.html

"In 1876, Pleasant Valley's first newspaper, the Pleasant Valley Bulletin, reported that the old armory was moved from its former location above the covered bridge to a new site on the north side of lower Main Street, known as McLaury's General Store. Later on, when this building became Pultz's General Store, it also served as the Pleasant Valley Post Office with John E. Laird as the Post Master, who was appointed on February 12, 1915.

In 1913, the tax records show George E. Pultz as the owner of "House and Store, north side Main Street, west by Millie Schneider, east by Depot Road, assessed at $1100".

Mrs. Ethel Cole, appointed June 26, 1935 and the only Pleasant Valley Post Mistress, first served when the Post Office was located in this building.

It was known as Dunken Pultz's Drug Store until 1946, at which time the new owners named it the Pleasant Valley Department Store.

The Pleasant Valley Department Store is one of the last remaining small and independently owned department stores in the region.

The year was 1946, and Harold Hommel and Walter Bogatis had recently become civilians. They had each served five years in the U.S. Army and had risen to the ranks of First Sergeant and Master Sergeant, respectively. Soon after the war ended, Hommel became involved in a partnership in the camera and accessory business in Poughkeepsie, NY. He had been in the photographic unit in the service, so he was very knowledgeable about the merchandise and a real asset to the business. Bogatis joined Hommel here after he left the service since he too had been involved in photography in the Army.

Soon, another opportunity arose for the two men. They met a woman who had a small town drugstore for sale. She had purchased the business (located in Pleasant Valley) from a licensed pharmacist who she had then hired, but was no longer interested in running it. Having decided that this was a great opportunity for them, Hommel and Bogatis scraped together the money they needed to buy the business from her. Their agreement was that the pharmacist would stay on and the business would be a pharmacy (with some general merchandise).

Also, they signed an assignable lease which carried the option to purchase the store building and property at an attractive figure.

The men decided to organize as a partnership, with everything split evenly. This agreement was written down and registered in the county clerk's office. On September 10, 1946, the Pleasant Valley Drug Store opened its doors for business.

The initial capital (under 5000) went towards the purchase of the business, merchandise, and beginning operating cash. Things went along smoothly until it was realized that the arrangement with the pharmacist was not going to work out, although he had been very helpful to them. He took his leave from the business and from that point on, they carried drugs under a state license to operate without a pharmacist but under authorization to fill prescriptions.

Soon they evolved into a general store, with more general merchandise and a soda fountain, while retaining the license to dispense drugs without a pharmacist. They still had not hired any help and did all the work themselves. They tried to carefully analyze what the people in the community wanted and could afford, and bought merchandise accordingly. The fountain was very successful and seemed to draw a lot of people into the store.

They became one of the biggest outlets around for Breyers Ice Cream, and they also made their own syrups. Very little advertising was done, except for a small handbill that they put in mailboxes and gave to customers as they came in. They still heavily relied on word-of-mouth as their main source of advertising. The store was located on a heavily traveled road, and their hours were 8am to 9pm.

Things went along this way until a pharmacist came to town in 1951 who wanted to start a business. This voided the Pleasant Valley Drug license, so the drug sales were discontinued and the general merchandise was expanded. Since 1946 they had a flashing neon sign in the front of the store that read "DRUGS", the new druggist however requested that the sign be taken down. Fearing the loss of customers they decided to turn off the "D" in drugs and have the sign read "RUGS". This move helped to keep customers coming in and they also sold a lot of rugs. The name of the business soon changed to the Pleasant Valley Department Store, and the neon sign was replaced with one that blinked "OPEN".

Some ideas worked and some didn't. They expanded on some lines and discontinued others. In 1953, they decided that they could do without the fountain, and could use the space to stock clothing. They still depended on word-of-mouth for their advertising, although they did have a few radio spots advertising thermal boots. They also began painting signs on the building to advertise the goods that they carried. In the years to come they expanded their clothing business and went heavily into the sporting goods, while still retaining the general store image. People said you could always find what you wanted at the Pleasant Valley Department Store, so always look there first.

The partners feel like they have succeeded because they know how important their relationships with the customers are, and how to keep a trustworthy image. Hommel passed away in 1996. The business is presently owned and operated by Hommel's daughter Caroline Dolfi. The partners have retired."

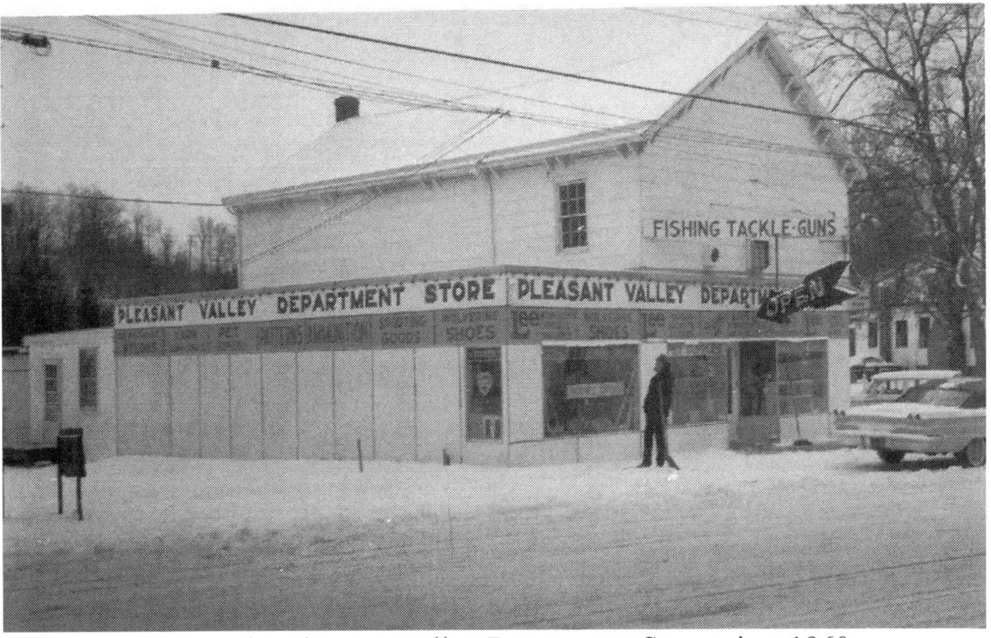

The Pleasant Valley Department Store, circa 1960

The owners of the Pleasant Valley Department Store, Walter Bogatis and Harold Hommel were both skilled photographers. they sold fishing bait and artificial lures for fishing. when fisherman were successful they sometimes came back to the store to show their catch and have their pictures taken.

Walter "Walt" P. Bogatis one of the owners of the Pleasant Valley Department Store, showing off his catch. (CD)

Harold Hommel one of the owners of the Pleasant Valley Department Store, showing off his catch. (CD)

Edna Hommel, Harold's wife, showing off her catch. (CD)

A local Pleasant Valley man and happy customer, Archie Smith showing off his catch.(CD)

The Masons

Masonic Lodge on Main Street as it looked in the 1980's (GBG)

Shekomeko Lodge No. 458 Free and Accepted Masons held the first communication at Mabbettsville on July 28, 1858. The Charter was granted August 18, 1859. Meetings were held over the Blacksmith shop. After a few years the Lodge was moved to Washington Hollow and continued to meet there until a fire destroyed the Temple in 1925. The Lodge then met at the Millbrook Masonic Temple for two years.

In 1927 the Lodge leased the Pleasant Valley Methodist Church and used the building jointly with the Church until 1951, at which time the Lodge purchased the building. When that building was sold and torn down to provide parking for the new fire house, they met in the Grange building on Quaker Hill Road.

2006 Shekomeko Masonic Lodge purchased the property at 3 Quaker Hill Road to build a lodge. The Dutchess County district, currently consists of a total of eleven separate lodges. Within this lodge building there are a total of five organizations currently meeting; Shekomeko F & AM, Beacon F & AM, Pleasant Valley Grange, Demolay (www.nydemolay.org) and Rainbow Girls (www.nyiorg.org). The Demolay and and Rainbow girls are two of the Masonic youth organizations that exist.

> Shekomeko is committed to assisting the world around them on both a local as well as a national and even international level. Locally, they are active sponsors of youth athletic programs, food banks, Boy Scouts of America, Girl Scouts of America, Castle Point veterans hospital visitations and the New York State Masonic Child Identification Program. This nationally recognized program is a service offered free of charge at a variety of locations throughout the year such as the Dutchess County Fair, and Pleasant Valley Days community day as well as many other venues. The Child ID program has already saved several children and is their way to help make the world a safer place. On a national and international level the New York State Mason's support the Masonic Brotherhood Fund, which contributions go to such causes as Medical Research through our own Masonic Medical Research facility (www.mmrl.edu), various military outreach programs as well as unfortunate causes that arise such as the September 11, 2001 terrorist attacks or national hurricane relief just to name a few.[gg]

ORDER OF THE EASTERN STAR

After Shekomeko Lodge moved to Pleasant Valley, Cecil Sherow, Lewis Erhart, Theodore Cross and other members convinced some of the ladies they should have an Eastern Star Chapter.

On January 13, 1928, a meeting was held at the home of Mr. and Mrs. Charles Cole on the south side of Main Street. Mrs. Erhart, a Vassar Chapter member; Mrs. Cole, and several other ladies had planned well and before adjournment were ready to receive prospective members. Mrs. Erhart suggested the name of Shekomeko Chapter. On March 6 Henrietta Fraleigh and Dr. Oliver, district officers, and Vassar Chapter's officers met in the Lodge rooms to organize, exemplify the Star work, and initiate the thirty members. On March 20th the first stated meeting of Shekomeko Chapter under Dispensation was held. Mr. and Mrs. Erhart, Matron and Patron, presided. Our first picnic on July Fourth was held at the home of Mr. and Mrs. John Plass at Rochdale. Mr. Plass was a member of Vassar Chapter, but because of time and effort given in helping Shekomeko, he was made an Honorary member and called the "Daddy" of Shekomeko Chapter. On November 26, 1928, Shekomeko Chapter #815 was granted its Charter.

The Pleasant Valley Grange building where the Masons met after they left Main Street. circa 1990's Picture taken from North Avenue (GBG)

The Pleasant Valley Grange building, picture taken from Quaker Hill Road. circa 2000 (TerriG)

The building built by the Masons 2006 after they purchased the land from the Grange. This picture was taken from North Avenue.

The current Shekomeko Lodge Masonic Hall built 2006, taken from Quaker Hill Road.

The Methodist Church

The church as it looked November 20, 1938 (HMJ)

The Pleasant Valley Methodist Church began as a preaching point, served by circuit preachers in the Dutchess County Circuit, 1788. Cornelius Cook and Andrew Harpending were the traveling preachers assigned to this circuit. They formed an organization to collect people into a little school house about a mile east of the village (known later as the Crow Hill School House). On July 27, 1825, this society bought one acre of land from James Odell for $150 on the road we now know as Route 44. They proceeded to build a church forty feet square and two and a half stories high. The deed of this property was given to William Dize, Solomon Sleight and William Harris as trustees.

A newspaper notice from the Poughkeepsie Journal announces a meeting of the Temperance Society at the Methodist Episcopal Church on February 13th, 1835.

Notice.

☞The friends of TEMPERANCE will please take notice that a simultaneous meeting of the Temperance Society, will be held at the Methodist Episcopal Church, in the Upper village of Pleasant Valley, on the evening of the 26th inst. at 6 o'clock.
Dated Pleasant Valley, Feb. 13th, 1835.
2w87 Z. N. HOFFMAN, Sec'y.

After the split from the Church of England in the 18th century the Church was known as the Methodist Episcopal Church. That is the church that served Pleasant Valley in the 19th and early 20th century. In 1939, it became the Methodist Church and in 1968, the United Methodist church.

That Methodist Church building was moved about one mile west into the center of the hamlet in 1845. The only thing that remains at this spot is a Methodist Cemetery, which is periodically cleaned up by volunteer groups. The covered bridge that spanned the Wappingers Creek at the time was too narrow for the building to fit, so it was taken down South Avenue about a quarter mile and brought across a shallow part of the creek and back east along the Filkintown road to the spot where it was to stay for over one hundred years. This detour added about a half mile to the move.

A picture of the church taken in 1915 shows the church as it looked on Main Street, with a box in front for ladies to step on to get down from their wagons. A stone foundation was added to raise the building up above the flood plain.

Picture during the time of Mason's ownership.

The Shekomeko Lodge, No. 458, Free and Accepted Masons, purchased the Main Street Church, and the deed was turned over to them in 1951. In 1949, the first plans for a new church were made. In 1953 the site for the new church on Martin Road was purchased from Mr. and Mrs. Gadlin Bodner.

The building, pictured above, that had housed the church and Masonic Lodge was torn down 2002 to make a parking lot for the Fire Station. A small monument was to be erected at the site in recognition of the Masonic Lodge.

Current Methodist Church on Martin Road.

With the help of an active youth group, who helped paint the inside of the new church, the opening of the newly constructed church building was held December 15, 1954. In 1962 more property was purchased from Mr. Bodner and a parsonage was erected. Reverend Furnival and family moved in May 31, 1963.

The congregation is very active, housing a food pantry and coordinating distribution of donations from local churches of non-perishable food items, paper products and cleaning supplies collected at local churches and distributed by the church members every Wednesday evening to meet community needs. The church also runs a Christian Nursery School.

The Methodist Cemetery on Route 44 has been cleaned up by Boy Scouts and other civic groups over the years. During 2011 the Briggs Auto Body shop cleaned it and straightened the stones where they could.

Methodist Cemetery, picture taken spring 2012. (PH)

Methodist Cemetery, picture taken spring 2012. (PH)

For a list of names of individuals interred in this cemetery see Appendix Methodist.

The Quakers

The Quakers came to the area that would later be the Town of Pleasant Valley in 1802. They first met for their worship services in private homes, principally in the home of Jonathan Dean. They established a boarding and day school at the house that is currently 1667 Main Street in 1809.

In 1810 they build a Meeting House near the corner of North Avenue and Quaker Hill Road in Pleasant Valley, that meeting was discontinued in 1881.

Quaker meeting house on Quaker Hill Road near North Avenue, circa 1812 (GBG)

The Quakers believed that Christ was revealed in every individual through a gift known as the inward light. Revelations came not from listening to sermons or prayers but from opening one's eyes to "that of God" within. Religious services, called meetings, in churches, or meetinghouses consisted of spontaneous testimonies of the inner light by those present, sometimes under the guidance of a pastor. Most meetings were not programmed. Members sat silently until they were moved to rise, voice a revelation, and then sit down.

The Pleasant Valley Quakers went to monthly meetings at the Oswego

Friends Meeting house, in the town of Beekman, about 14 miles away. The road they took to get to that meeting house is the road that is called South Avenue and Freedom Road now. At that time it was referred to as the "Road to Oswego."

According to a town legend, Timothy Farrington, a well-known Friend, lived on South Avenue and had a saw mill along the Wappingers Creek. He supplied the community with much needed lumber. One year, due to a long drought, the creek was too low to run the saw. At last rain came and Timothy ran his mill on Sunday. The Presbyterian pastor objected strongly to Timothy sawing on Sunday, but Timothy said "The good Lord sent the rain and he expects me to make use of it while it lasts and boards are needed." Shortly after this the pastor needed some boards. He went to Timothy but specified that the boards should not be those sawed on Sunday. Timothy obliged and hunted out other boards. When the pastor paid for his boards, Timothy remarked, "I do hope this money isn't any thee earned by working on Sunday."

Another story is of a well known Quaker mill owner was Daniel Dean, who built the Bowman Mill in 1810. He produced cloth that was blue with spots of white paste for variety. Being a good Quaker, he would guarantee that the blue color was permanent, or fast, but he warned that the white paste just might wash out. Needless to say, it always did. The mill itself, unlike the cloth it produced, was not guaranteed and it burned down in 1848, was rebuilt, and burned again in 1915, never to run again.

In 1922 the Quakers sold the Pleasant Valley Meeting House, but not the burial ground to the Pleasant Valley Grange. In 1946 they sold another unused portion of the grounds to the Pleasant Valley Grange. The property is currently owned by the Shekomeko Masonic Lodge of Pleasant Valley. In 2006 the Masonic lodge built a new building, the Pleasant Valley Grange also meets in that building.

Here is a sample of four of the stones from the Quaker Cemetery.

According to "Old Gravestones of Dutchess County, New York" by J. W. Poucher, published in 1924, the most recent stone in the Quaker Cemetery is 1913, most others are from 1800's.

For a list of names of individuals interred in this cemetery see Appendix Quaker.

House on the north side of Main Street just up the hill from the village, address, 1667 Main Street. Date and photographer unknown (GBG)

Israel Dean and Robert Abbot operated a boarding and day school from 1809 to 1819 in this house. Robert Abbot owned and operated the Pleasant Valley Finishing Mill at the time. The students embroidered maps of North and South America as part of their education.

This house was in the Husted family for over 100 years. During the early 1950's when Brownie and Albert Husted lived here, on Halloween the Trick or Treaters were invited in for treats.

Brownie had beautiful flower gardens around and behind the house. They had a black cook, named Georgie Moore, who lived in a small house about a quarter of a mile away on the right side of South Avenue overlooking the Wappingers Creek.

St. Paul's Episcopal Church

St. Paul's church circa 1911

Saint Paul's Church has had a long and active history in this old Dutchess County community. Physically, the church building itself has changed little since it was erected in 1842 at a cost of $1800 including the lot, with materials at hand. It is not unlike the miniature churches one sees as part of Christmas decorations, surrounded by old trees and approached by a charming path. The interior, as well as the exterior of the building is photogenic. Its builders remembered the cathedrals of the old country and reproduced the forms they knew and loved so well with such materials as were available. Three arched windows above the alter describe the larger arch reminiscent of a Gothic cathedral. The glass in these windows is American primitive stained glass. The passing of the years has not dulled the brilliant reds and blues of the glass.

The church was organized in 1837, although there had been missionary activities for some time before that. The first baptisms were recorded as of February 26, 1842, the first marriage recorded in the parish register was on May 28, 1842, and the first burial in May of the same year. The church yard, with headstones all facing toward the church, tell much of the history of Pleasant Valley and its first families. Names of many roads in the area correspond with family names in the old parish register: Traver, Sherow, Bower, Marshall, Travis, Vanderburgh, Drake and Masten.

St. Paul's Church with the parish house almost completed circa 1959

Clergy who have served the church in the past include The Reverend Richard Russell Upjohn from 1903-1912. He was listed in "Who's Who in New York" 1904 addition, page 597, he was the son of the architect who introduced Gothic revival architecture in this country, designing many churches including the present Trinity Church, Wall Street, New York City. The Reverend Walker Anderson Edwards, a native of England, was rector from 1913-1928. Before coming to Pleasant Valley he had, for fifteen years, been a missionary priest in the Diocese of Antigua, British West Indies. He is buried in Saint Paul's Churchyard. The priest-in-charge in 1963 was the Reverend John Prescott Miner, who was appointed to the church in October 1961 by the Bishop of New York. During the 1970's the priest was The Reverend Wayne Schmidt, he and his wife, Louise, had two boys, Wayne and David, to liven up the rectory. The current priest is The Reverend Ellen O'Hara.

The "Thrift Store", run by the women of the church is in the church basement and has been serving the community since the 1970's.

A new Parish House completed in 1959 serves the community as a meeting place for Girl Scouts, AA groups, and many other local groups. There is a youth group that is very active. They do lots of fun things, and are involved in helping the adults with their fund raising efforts.

The St. Patrick's Day corned beef and cabbage supper is an annual event attended by over a hundred hungry people who come from near and far. During the Pleasant Valley Weekend celebration in September members of the church have a chicken barbeque at the parish hall with family style servings during Saturday afternoon, with all you can eat chicken, potato salad, farm fresh tomatoes and corn, and delicious deserts baked by the parishioners. During the whole weekend celebration members of the church work in the specially built sausage and peppers trailer at the recreation park providing customers with friendly service and excellent sandwiches.

As you look out the window over the sink in the parish hall, at the top of little hill in the cemetery there is the large stone, engraved "Lovelace", it indicates the final resting place for my mother, father Uncle George, Aunt Nettie, cousin Maude, and a stone that marks the space for my ashes.

Saint Stanislaus Kostka Parish

Through the years it has been called, St. Stanislaus, St, Stan's or just "The Catholic Church in Pleasant Valley," but today it is referred to by its proper name, "Saint Stanislaus Kostka Parish."

In 1902, Roman Catholics in the Pleasant Valley vicinity wanted a church of their own. They met in a meeting hall in the carriage house on the property of the Michael Hoctor Hotel. That Hotel, across Main Street from the present church, was later know as Talbot's Inn and the 1830 Inn.

St. Stanislaus Roman Catholic Church c1912

A shrine church was started by Father Walsh, who was in charge of St. Andrews-on-Hudson. In 1912, a lot across the street was bought, on which was a wagon shop, that had been owned and operated by the Ten Hagen family. A church was built and named St. Stanislaus Kostka, in honor of the patron saint of St. Andrews-on-Hudson, a Jesuit Seminary along the Hudson River. That property now belongs to the Culinary Institute of America. During that time priests walked from Hyde Park to Pleasant Valley to serve mass.

Priests serving this parish have been: Father O'Brien, Father Moylan, Father Dunn, Father Nicholas, Father Richardson, Father Puglisis and Father Herlihy, all community minded men, who have made a distinct contribution not only to their church, but also to the village.

An article headlined "Negroes' Catholic Church To Be Built Here in Year" in the May 16, 1932 Poughkeepsie reported that St. Stanislaus church in Pleasant Valley joined with St. Mary's Church, Poughkeepsie to sponsor the project of building the first Roman Catholic Church in Poughkeepsie for Negroes. It further reported that about 125 negroes of Poughkeepsie, Hopewell Junction and Pleasant Valley attended the first formal service.

Over the years the entire community enjoyed the fund raising summer bazaars held on the large front lawn of the church.

Mr. and Mrs. Germiller were among the many parishioners who worked tirelessly at the church and during the bazaars, the last of July and first of August. Mr. Germiller used his vacation from DeLaval in Poughkeepsie to work on the bazaars. The manufacturing company closed those two weeks every summer. Mr. Germiller and other men built the booths. He also ran the "Big Six wheel." One could play any amount of money on one of six numbers and the wheel had dice painted on it in groups of three. If your number came up on any one of the three die, you won that number of coins back in the denomination you played. He did other fix up jobs around the church like kneeling benches, and he was an usher. Mrs. Germiller ran the doll booth. There was always a very large doll in the middle - the big prize. The chances were in punch cards, with a little poker-like thing you punched out on a card in a pleated piece of paper with a number on it. If the number corresponded with the number on the doll, you won. The dolls ranged from small (8 or ten inches) to large (20 to 30 inches). They were dressed beautifully - in a child's estimation anyway. Most were hard bodies. The "magic skin" dolls came later. Mrs. Germiller also started the first choir and helped clean the rectory when the housekeeper was on vacation.

On July 8, 1956, the cornerstone of the new church was laid following the 12 o'clock mass. The fellowship hall is named in honor of Father Dunne, beloved not only by his parishioners, but the entire community. He loved his work here, for he once said, "Here I can really be a shepherd to my flock."

The November 13, 1934 Poughkeepsie Journal reported a story of Father Dunne's service during World War I. Father Dunne was the war time Chaplin of the 306th Infantry Regiment of the 77th Division; he earned the Distinguished Service Cross during the war.

The stain glass windows from the mission church that sat perpendicular to the present church or where the church hall sits now were placed in the present church.

Father Richardson made a big difference in the church as he would charm the parishioners thanking them for their generosity and he built the present church. He was a former military chaplain and very "military" in his approach. At rehearsal he would have the wedding attendants and bride and groom kneel in a certain way during their procession. He'd say "cut the cross" which meant kneel right there with your back straight on the cross in the tile floor. His opinion was that weddings were a "holy show." He was well liked in Pleasant Valley and did a lot for the parish. He took the women who cleaned the church and made cancer dressing for Rosary Hill in Westchester to Broadway shows. He bought a station wagon and piled in the kids who went to Poughkeepsie parochial schools after the Arlington system no longer bused those kids outside the district. He took families to Lakeville, Connecticut to picnic and swim every summer. During the 1950's Father Richardson took groups of teenagers from the community to a swimming pool in Mabbettsville, near Millbrook, about ten miles away. He was there many years.

Monument that was placed on the northwest corner of the church property during the 1971 town sesquicentennial ceremony.

Saint Stanislaus Kostka Parish Church at it looked in 1963 and still looks as I write this book.

The Presbyterian Church of Pleasant Valley

PRESBYTERIAN CHURCH, PLEASANT VALLEY, N. Y.
PHOT. & PUB. BY L. S. HORTON, HYDE PARK, N. Y.

During 1765, in Pleasant Valley, Mr. Henry Lott was operating his mill near the "Great Bridge" and on November 12, a dedicated young man named Wheeler Case was installed as the first minister of the Pleasant Valley Presbyterian Church.

Mr. Case also ministered to the Poughkeepsie congregation for five years. In 1770 he asked to be released from his duties there, probably because a church had been erected in the village of Pleasant Valley on land deeded by Jacob and Margaret Everson for the consideration of ten shillings ($2.50). The first church building was a frame structure built about 4 rods (66 feet) southwest of the present church. The walls were unplastered, and there were no pews until 1786. The congregation used boards laid on blocks and benches for 16 years. The officers and choir sat beneath the high octagonal pulpit which was supported by a single wooden pillar.

Mr. Case also served the Pittsburg Church, which had been built in 1747, and was used as a barracks for Tories[6], and thus was badly in need of repairs when the troops departed the area. A band of nearly 400 Tories assembled at the Pittsburg church in the summer of 1777. They came principally from the southern part of the county and left the church in small parties for the bordering settlements where they intimidated the patriots and obtained supplies for the British Army. A company of American soldiers from Sharon, Connecticut surprised the Tories, killing several. About 30 others were captured and marched to Sharon. From there they were taken to New Hampshire and held until the end of the war. Later that church building became part of the Town of Washington. The cemetery located on the opposite side of the road from the church eventually became part of the Town of Pleasant Valley.

In 1821, the Town of Pleasant Valley was formed, and in 1829, the Presbyterian Church got a new minister, Benjamin F. Wile, who remained the minister there until 1867. Mr. Wile, a most persuasive and convincing speaker, was widely known as both an earnest advocate of Temperance and as a successful evangelist. He is credited with the almost entire abolishment of the liquor traffic from the neighborhood of Pleasant Valley during the mid-nineteenth century, having secured more than 5,000 signatures to the total abstinence pledge.

There is also a story that when Reverend Wile's son (the "baby" of the 150th Regiment of New York) mustered out at Poughkeepsie in 1865, Mr. Wile made a promise that he was delighted to keep. In bidding farewell to the regiment, he told them that when any man wished to get married, he'd perform the ceremony free of charge. It is said that the post-war years were not as profitable as others had been for the church, since quite a few homecoming veterans gladly accepted his offer.

By 1844, Methodist and Episcopal churches had been established in the village. Methodists, Episcopalians and Presbyterians often attended one another's services, and temperance meetings were held at all three churches. Entries in the diary of John Bower, local farmer and business man, made many references to temperance meetings which were sometimes held every night for a week's time, with different speakers being featured each evening.

[6] (tory) an American who favored the British side during the American Revolution. wordnetweb.princeton.edu/perl/webwn

Church and Manse about 1869, photographer unknown.

In 1860, a few members were dismissed from the Pleasant Valley Presbyterian Church to form the Westminster Church at Salt Point, and on January 12, 1861, more members were dismissed from Pleasant Valley to also join the Westminster Church.

About 1885, a committee was formed to recommend suitable action on the evils of Sunday newspapers. It was considered sinful to engage in any business activity on Sunday, including the sale of newspapers. However, no mention is found in the minutes of any action being taken on this matter. Around the beginning of the 19th century there is mention of offenses such as "frolicking" which was when a man rolled a hoop down Main Street on the Sabbath, and attending a dance which was populated "with wicked young people."

A new chapel, to be used mainly for Sunday school purposes was constructed in 1886. The cornerstone was laid on May 22, and contained several documents, with facts thought to be of interest, such as a list of the local businesses. Among these was a list of Sunday school teachers and students. There were 11 classes, and a note was made that "classes 3 and 4 were made up of colored children."

There was a paper prepared by Eli Mastin, Jr. which read as follows:

"Pleasant Valley, May 20, 1886

This village was incorporated in the year 1814 April 15. Adrean Post is the Contractor of this building. Carmon Osterhout, George Silvernail, George Rugar, Isaac Turner, and Eli Mastin, Jr. These are all the men worked on the brick and stone.

William Cronkrite is Boss Carpenter. There are three stores in the Village. One kept by Mr. Wright Devine, one by Mr. Wm. S. Smith, Edward C. Drake and Albert Devine.

There is one temperance hotel kept by Mr. Wm. C. Armstrong also he is a dealer in coal.

Two Blacksmith shops, one kept by Mr. John S. VanKeuren, one by Mr. John S. Spaulding. One Tin Shop kept by Frank P. Lasher (donor of box for corner stone) one Grist Mill kept by George Bordman, Sr. One Cotton Mill, Edward Farrington, Superintendent. James Farrington, Bookkeeper. Three Doctors, Dr. Irving D. LeRoy, Dr. Frank P. Wilson and Dr. Traver. Also Mr. Wright Devine is Postmaster. Edward Drake Supervisor, Harvey Bullock, Town Clerk, Ezra Holmes, Collector, Edward Ackerman, Commissioner of Highways, he also keeps a Livery Stable. Wm. H. Smith, Carpet Weaver, Elisha Wolvin keeps a Meat Market. James VanKleck, Wm. VanKeuren and Wm. Hunt peddle milk. Wm. H. Smith is Agent for the Sunday Courier. Charles Cady for the Utica Globe and James Palmateer for the Albany Telegram, Hiram Wright, Cigars and Candy peddler. Eli Mastin Sr. Peddles drugs and medicine. Sidney Mastin, Wm Lewis and Theodore Beneway are the painters.

There are three school teachers. Miss Alice Kay teacher in Dist. No. 2, Miss Regina Mills in Dist. No. 3 and Elvena Colwell in Dist, No. 4. Geo. H. Hooper, Ticket Agent and Telegraph Operator. Samuel Moore, Section Boss. Oliver Y. Haviland, Harness Maker, Jonas B. Cross, Pastor of M. E. Church, Wm. Bower President of the Board of Health.

Gotten up by Eli Mastin, Jr."[hh]

It is also recorded that an outbreak of polio in Pleasant Valley forced the Sunday school to close for seven Sundays in July and August of 1916, and a severe epidemic of influenza during the winter of 1918, making it necessary to postpone the annual Meeting and close the church for some weeks. On November 5, 1919, Pleasant Valley voted in favor of prohibition by 200 votes. A representative from the "Anti-Saloon League" spoke at a morning service in the church in 1920, and the WCTU (Women's Christian Temperance Union) held several meetings, including its annual convention there.

During the late 1880's, a cemetery association was formed, a new organ was installed and new hymn books were purchased, and the horse shed was enlarged.

Presbyterian Cemetery looking from the front of the church, circa 1994

Presbyterian Cemetery looking from the cemetery toward the church, circa 1994

The church was expanded July, 1956, to provide classroom space for 350 children. In preparation for the erection of the new building, it was necessary to demolish the chapel, which had been built in 1886. The old records were found in the box they had been placed in, they were replaced in the corner stone and put in the wall of the new building on December 16, 1956, along with several current items. A new fellowship hall was dedicated, the "Chester Husted Memorial Fellowship Hall" after a life-long member of the church. Mr. Agnew, the minister at the time stated, "It might be considered an historical event for the Pleasant Valley Church that on March 20, 1957, Session granted the Junior High Fellowship permission to hold a dance in the fellowship hall - the money to be donated to the building fund."

In 1955 the first women were installed as elders, and a trustee. In 1959 the first women became deacons.

The church was enlarged again in 1963, to add more classroom space. Over the years the Manse has been sold to the library, the church was made handicap accessible with the installation of a lift in the front of the church[ii].

The Church currently is involved with the Homeless Shelter in Poughkeepsie, provides food for the Pleasant Valley Food Pantry, and supports CROP Walk, the Rural and Migrant Ministry, as well as the Foundation for Religious and Mental Health. They also provide support to the Lunch Box in

Poughkeepsie through the donation of groceries and volunteering time for the preparation of meals for people in need.

The Bargain Basement is a thrift store located in our Church, which helps to support many programs and charities. [jj]

Westminster Presbyterian Church

Westminster Presbyterian Church, circa 1963

A commission, appointed by the Presbytery of the North River, met with 17 persons in Salt Point on December 20, 1860, to discuss the formation of the Westminster Presbyterian church; the church was incorporated on May 28, 1861.

Over $3000.oo was raised by subscription toward the $3408.00, which was the final cost of the building. On October 24, 1961, a fair was held with the proceeds going to finish the building. There were 29 parishioners. Although the church construction was financed by subscription the pastor's salary and other operating expenses were met by pew rentals. The pews were rented for a year with the 6 center front pews going for $12.50. Some of the renters were delinquent in their payments and it was necessary to canvass the congregation to collect back rents, as well as to accept notes payable at 11%. In 1890 it was decided to introduce the envelope pledging system that is still in use today. Pastors' salaries varied from $500.00 to $800.00 per year, including the use of a manse. Over the years several manses were acquired and sold. The current manse on Salt Point Turnpike was built in the late 1950's by Ralph Wilbur.

In 1887-88 plans were started to add a chapel to the rear of the church; fairs and festivals were held to raise money for this project.

At the beginning of this century the church became an integral part of the community; not only by caring for the spiritual needs of the members, but by supporting Boy and Girl Scout troops, a Young People's Christian Endeavor Society, Vacation Bible School and a Missionary Society.

By 1928 the church became self supporting and no longer required financial aid from Presbytery.

The church was erected in 1861, with its pointed steepled roof, tripled gabled porch and ornate bracketed eaves is an excellent example of Gothic Revival architecture in the Victorian era. It has been called "Carpenter Gothic."

In February 1983 a fire, of suspicious nature, totally destroyed this fine building. Shortly after the fire it was decided to rebuild the church following the original lines, without the chapel but having a full basement. Through the efforts of the congregations, friends of the church, the community, BOCES[7] and many other individuals and foundations over $250,000.00 was raised. It took about 3 years. The new building has risen from the ashes and the congregation was once again worshipping at Westminster Church on the Salt Point Turnpike in the Hamlet of Salt Point, New York.

Almost everyone in the congregation, young and older, worked diligently on the many fund raising projects. Three people have spent many, many hours working on the rebuilding. Gladys Horne composed and wrote every letter that was sent soliciting funds for the church; "Gil" Halstead drew up the plans and worked with the contractors and BOCES; John Richie, the treasurer, not only helped raise the funds but invested them to receive the optimum return. He also helped "Gil" in many ways.

No history of Westminster would be complete without mentioning the women's Circle, or Women's Auxiliary as it was once named; they have worked to raise money for church project and also give generously to the

[7] Boards of Cooperative Education Services

Presbyterian Mission program.

A church service is not complete without music and the church is indebted to Ethel Timmer who has been the organist and choir director, for many years. She is also the director of the bell choir.

The church has remained small but vibrant. Membership is around 50, and has graduated to part time stated supply ministers, the current pastor is the Reverend Ted Miller. The church continues to be a beacon for the community and surrounding area.

Westminster Presbyterian Church, circa 2012 (TS)

The Central Baptist Church

CENTRAL BAPTIST CHURCH
Picture taken 1963

In the words of Central Baptist Church:

"In the beginning God created the heaven and the earth. Even then God knew the times, the places and the events leading up to the birth of **Central Baptist Church**.

On June 24, 1869, in a small village called Bloomvale, a new chapel was dedicated as a branch of the Dutch Reformed Church at South Millbrook. Eventually, this building became the future home of Central Baptist Church.

The forerunners and founders of Central Baptist Church were people who came from Virginia to work on Dutchess County farms. Some of them were relatives and friends who had attended Hope Church in Virginia. After worshipping on Sunday afternoon with their friends at church in Clinton Corners, with the assistance of Reverend A. W. Farmer of Poughkeepsie, a Mission was formed and called New Hope Baptist Mission, being a namesake of Hope Church in Virginia.

The former Dutch Reformed building was unoccupied and was being used as a storage place for farm machinery and hay. The members of the Mission decided to talk to Mr. Edwin Sweezy, the owner of the building, about holding services there. The result was a rental agreement with the consideration of one cent per month and a lengthy set of stipulations. Brother sank Morton, Brother Clem Hancock, Brother Armistead Walls and Brother Walter Coleman signed the agreement on the first day of December 1916. The new congregation held services there starting in the spring of 1917, with a very small membership; the people had a mind to work. Sunday school was held every Sunday morning. Prayer and preaching service were held in the afternoon. The first revival was held in the fall of 1917, with Reverend W. E. Jones as the revivalist. As a result 15 people were added to the membership of the Mission. On Sunday, May 11, 1919, the New Hope Baptist Mission was organized into the Central Baptist Church of Clinton Corners, NY. Reverend E. W. Ellis was our spiritual leader during this time. This was our church home for 70 years until it was damaged by fire in 1987 and demolished two years later to be converted into our parking lot.

The Reverend Frank H. Wiggins was called as our first permanent pastor and served for 20 years. It was under his administration that we bought the church building and at a later date the lot that the building stood on. The total cost was $1,000.00. It was no easy task during the depression times when money was virtually nonexistent.

On Saturday, February 25, 1922, the church was incorporated with three trustees: Brother Charles Duke, Brother Harry Braddock and Brother Armistead Wells. Present at that meeting were Reverend Frank Wiggins, Justice of the Peace Newton Fowler and 17 church members. In 1939, Reverend Charles E. Boyd assumed the Pastorate on the recommendation of Reverend Wiggins, who had resigned. Reverend Byrd's tenure was interrupted by service as a Chaplain in the US Army. During his absence Reverend Samuel Hodge faithfully served the congregation as Interim Pastor. In 1947 Reverend Roger L. Douglas began a ten-year term as Pastor. He was instrumental in establishing a Deaconess Ministry and in re-organizing the Senior and Youth Choirs. In December of 1957, Reverend Robert D. Dixon was called and served 19 years. During his tenure many structural changes were made, including an addition with a meeting hall, indoor plumbing and a Baptismal pool. The membership grew tremendously. Reverend Melvin J. Roundtree became Pastor in 1978 and served almost 17 years until God called him to his eternal home. During this period the adjacent parsonage together with ample space for the building of the existing place of worship was dedicated on August 20, 1989.

On February 4, 1998, Reverend Richard Preston Butler, Sr., Servant of God, was called to be Pastor. Through the preaching and teaching of his willing vessel, our congregation has continued to grow spiritually and additional ministries have been formed. In the eight years that we been under Pastor Butler's, many upgrades have been completed in and around our church. He has lead the church in obtaining its 501© 3 status, as well as purchasing a church van and 9.5 acres of land. Many new members have been added, choirs have been reorganized, a new copier has been obtained, our church motto has changed, and a Tuesday morning Bible Study has been added. This year God blessed us with the consecrating of four Servant Leaders to the office of the Deaconess Ministry and Brother Kevin Moore as Servant Leader to the Office of the Deacon Ministry; with the 'Spirit of Expectancy' we are continuing to move onward and upward!

'To God Be The Glory' "

Copied directly from letter of Lillie Cooper, member of the congregation of the Central Baptist Church.

Central Baptist Church, picture from church. circa 2010

Central Baptist Church, picture from church. circa 2010

Netherwood Baptist Church

The Netherwood Baptist church as it looked before it burned.

While maintaining its identity as a county Baptist Church, the little white church near Salt Point, about 6 miles from the center of the hamlet of Pleasant Valley, extends friendly service to all the surrounding community. Since its organization over 200 years ago, this church has maintained a distinct place in the history of rural churches in Dutchess County. Searching through old incomplete church records, it was found that through the 1770's Elder John Lawrence was followed by Elder Comer Bullock, an evangelist. He preached near Salt Point around 1791. At that time some of the members broke away to form their own organization, the Bangall Church, in a town about 10 miles northeast. In 1790 a one-half acre parcel of land was deeded to the church by John Van Voorhis. By 1795 Elder John Dodge was called as pastor and served the church until 1813. In 1842 Elder Philip Roberts became pastor of the Netherwood Church. Several improvements were made, a public shed and barn erected, and parsonage remodeled. The old grave yard of the church, contains many stone slabs dating as far back as 1794.

In 1901 the name of the church was changed from the Pleasant Valley Church to the present name of Netherwood Baptist Church. Thirty pastors served the church from the time when Elder Dodge was Pastor up to 1963. Many improvements were made in the 1950's including the enlargement of the church hall with rest rooms. According to deed records in the Dutchess County Office Building, Market Street, Poughkeepsie, New York, Libre 14, Page 132, dated June 7, 1796. John Van Voorhis and his wife Hannah sold one half acre of land between their house and the house of Anthony Badgley for the sum of five pounds to the Baptist church for the use of a meetinghouse for worship and a burial ground for the Baptist Church, their trustees and successors. The paperwork notes that when the Baptist Church does not require or stand in need of the meetinghouse, any regular Minister of the Church of England or Presbyterians or Congregationalists may use the building.

The Pastor in 2010 is Elizabeth Travis Clarkson. Services are still held every Sunday in the new church that was built after the old church burned around 1995 or 2000. The congregation at this time numbers about 100.

Netherwood Baptist Church as it looks today.(from church bulletin)

Key to Appendix

Reference information for "Interments in the FRIENDS' GROUND" and "Interments in the METHODIST GROUND".

Prior to 1880 registration of vital statistics was occasional or more often, entirely neglected. In general, the editors have omitted stones bearing date in the latter portion of the nineteenth century. The gathering of these inscriptions was begun in April, 1911, and was practically finished in the autumn of 1916 but the World War delayed publication.

The use of brackets indicates uncertainty as to the lettering on the stone. Lists are arranged alphabetically, first by family names, second by the Christian names in one family.

b.	=	Born	wid.	=	Widow
d.	=	Died, Day, Days	a	=	age
dau.	=	Daughter	y.	=	year, years
s.	=	Son	m.	=	Month, Months
w.	=	Wife			

Civil War Appendix:

Names and other information was gathered from these sources:

Pages 319 & 320 of History of Duchess County, New York

www.Ancestry. com records and records on line of 150th & 128th Regiments

(TC) Microfilm covering the period from 15th day of April, 1861 to the date of the certificate of the town clerk

History of the 128th Regiment by David Hanaburgh

Regiment (128 or 150) rank and age from Pleasant Valley historical files from University of NY State Education Department, Albany, NY

If men were paid a "Mustering in" bonus, and the amount was given on the microfilm roster I listed it. The wages were to be $13 per month, it is not clear if it was paid.

http://www.rootsweb.ancestry.com/~nydutche/cems/method.htm

Interments in the METHODIST GROUND

"Old Gravestones of Dutchess County, New York" by J. W. Poucher published in 1924, pages 223-226.

Note: Some of Poucher's listings have been found to be inaccurate, so use these with caution. If you find any inaccuracies in this listing please send them to me so that I may correct them. Lynn Brandvold (lynnb@nmt.edu) Thanks.

CLASSIFICATION: Churchyard.
LOCATION: East of the village of Pleasant Valley, on the north side of the main highway.
CONDITION: Overgrown; surrounded by a stone wall.
INSCRIPTIONS: 175 in number. Copied October 4,1913, by J. W. Poucher, M. D., and Mrs. Poucher.
REMARKS: In 1825 Methodists in Pleasant Valley built a church on this site. The building was removed to the village in 1845.

1. Allen, Lucy, w. of Israel, d. 1864, Feb. 26, a. 53 y.
2. Babcock, Frank, s. of William & Phebe, d. 1887, July 26, in 26th y.
3. Babcock, Laura, dau. of William & Phebe, d. 1866, May 10, a. 6-7-16.
4. Banks, Ann Storms, w. of Daniel W., d. 1858, Mar. 27, a. 64-1-15.
5. Banks, Daniel W., d. 1859, May 30, a. 59-4-17.
6. Banks, Joseph W., s. of Daniel W. & Ann, d. 1839, Mar. 2, a. 1-9-29.
7. Bartlett, Armenia A. Wesley, w. of Charles B., d. 1861, Nov. 11, a. 29-11-18.
8. Beadle, Elisha, d. 1841, June 9, a. 62-11-9.
9. Birch, George, d. 1833, June 8, a. 57 y.
10. Birch, Rachel, w. of George, d. 1865, July 10, a. 81-4-12.
11. Bishop, Bartlett, Co. B, 128th N. Y. S. V., d. 1903, Mar. 26, a. 78 y.
12. Bishop, Charles A., d. 1867, Jan. 15, a. 2 y. 4 m.
13. Bishop, Ellen M., d. 1872, May 6, a. 15 y.

14. Bishop, Frederick A., d. 1864, June 3, a. 9-6-8.
15. Bishop, Uphemia Cole, w. of Bartlett, d. 1890, May 21, a. 66 y.
16. Bishop, William T., s. of Jacob S. & Sarah, d. 1863, July 26, a. 2 m. 16 d.
17. Bodenshatz, Louisa, dau. of John & Mary, d. 1867, Sep. 11, a. 3-8-17.
18. Bullock, Catharine, d. 1849, May 4, in 89th y.
19. Bullock, Mary, w. of Israel, d. 184(0), Feb. 13, a. 65 y. 9 m.
20. Burtis, Marie, dau. of Garret S. & Mary, d. 1849, May 31, in 25th y.
21. Cantine, Lucy, w. of Aaron, d. 1867, Jan. 25, a. 52-9-22.
22. Cheesman, Caroline L., w. of Filkins, d. 1850, Nov. 10, a. 51 y. 12 d.
23. Cheesman, Jacob, d. 1869, Nov. 16, a. 40 y. 11 d.
24. Cheesman, John N., s. of Filkins, d. 1831, Jan. 12, a. 7 y. 13 d.
25. Clark, Christiana T., dau. of Robert & Eliza, d. 1845, Aug. 15, a. 11 m. 15 d.
26. Clark, Eliza, w. of Robert, d. 1883, Mar. 21, a. 78-2-21.
27. Clark, Robert, d. 1862, Jan. 9, a. 69 y.
28. Collins, Oliver D., d. 1833, Feb. 13, a. 55 y. 2 m.
29. Collins, Oliver Davis, b. 1816, June 14, d. 1887, Sep. 16.
30. Collins, Sarah Ward, w. of Oliver D., d. 1860, Oct. 25, a. 76-8-13.
31. Cramer, Abraham, d. 1861, Mar. 3, a. 62 y. 15 d.
32. Cramer, Abraham, s. of Abraham & Permilla, d. 1875, Apr. 29, at Utica, N. Y., a. 39-7-21.
33. Cramer, Elizabeth Dingee, w. of Israel, d. 1866, Dec. 7, a. 74-3-18.
34. Cramer, Permilla, w. of Abraham, d. 1849, Feb. 17, a. 48-2-5.
35. Cramer, Sarah, d. 1886, Oct. 7, a. 64 y.
36. Crume, Lauretta Ann, w. of John P., d. 1851, Nov. 13, a. 49 y. 2 m.
37. Dean, Catherine M., d. 1856, June 16, in 26th y.
38. Dennis, William H., Co. C, 159th N. Y. (no dates).
39. Dise, William, d. 1851, Jan. 23, a. 80 y.
40. Doughty, John H., d. 1879, Aug. 20, a. 26-6-26.
41. DuBois, John R., d. 1872, July 23, a. 61 y.
42. DuBois, Rebecca, w. of John R., d. 1858, Jan. 3, a. 38-4-19.
43. Edmonds, Kerinada, d. 1857, Nov. 23, a. 33 y.
44. Elliott, Joseph H., s. of Rev. Joseph & Harriet M., d. 1856, Sep. 28, a. 6 m. 9 d.
45. Estelle, Helen Bishop, w. of John, b. 1834, July 4, d. 1902, Jan. 12.
46. Estelle, John, b. 1839, Jan. 1, d. 1902, Feb. 11.
47. Flagler, Maria E., dau. of Stephen & Caroline, d. 1845, Mar. 8, a. 6-10-9.
48. Flagler, Mary S., dau. of Stephen & Caroline, d. 1850, Sep. 2, a. 2 y. 9 d.
49. Foster, Elizabeth, d. 1857, Nov. 20, a. 81 y.
50. Foster, Frances A., d. 1873, Mar. 20, a. 30 y.
51. Foster, John I., d. 1852, Feb. 9, in 75th y.
52. Fowler, Ellen S., d. 1877, Sep. 9, a. 69 y.

53. Fowler, Senekey, d. 1856, Aug. 28, in 56th y.
54. (Gentleman), Mary, w. of James, d. 1849, May 19, a. 40 y. 8 m.
55. Giraud, Ann E.. dau. of Frederick & Margaret, d. 1861, June 3, a. 15 m. 3 d.
56. Graham, Angeline, w. of Richard, b. 1835, Feb. 18, d. 1871, Jan. 21.
57. Harris, Elizabeth, w. of William, d. 1829, Sep. 12, a, 54-11-7.
58. Harris, George C., d. 1837, May 5, a. 26 y. 24 d.
59. Harris, William, d. 1828, Feb. 18, a. 51-10-10.
60. Hart, Sarah, w. of William, d. 1858, Mar. 11, a. 66-11-20.
61. Hill, Gabriel, d. 1855, July 16, a. 67-2-11.
62. Hill, Owen S., d. 1892, Mar. 16, a. 53 y.
63. Hill, Sarah A., w. of Gabriel, b. 1810, Mar. 20, d. 1880, June 3.
64. Horton, Benjamin, b. 1836, Feb. 14, d. 1855, June 11.
65. Horton, Mamie, dau. of Benjamin & Jane, d. 1880, Dec. 21, a. 5-3-20.
66. Horton, Mary Jane Robertson, w. of Benjamin, b. 1838, Mar. 19, d. 1911, Oct. 6.
67. Howard, Hezekiah, d. 1849, May 13, in 44th y.
68. Howard, John W., s. of William & Pauline, d. 1848, Dec. 3, a. 1-4-20.
69. Howard, Maria, w. of Hezekiah, d. 1870, Dec. 4, in 59th y.
70. Howard, Paulina Storms, w. of William, d. 1867, Apr. 6, a. 62 y. 6 m.
71. Husted, Phebe J., w. of James D., d. 1860, Oct. 3, a. 37-4-27.
72. Ingraham, Anna Thorn, w. of John L., d. 1859, Sep. 19, a. 74-7-27.
73. Ingraham, Gilbert, s. of Gilbert H. & Mary P., d. 1852, June 27, a. 5 m.
74. Ingraham, Gilbert H., d. 1852, May 27, a. 31-7-20.
75. Ingraham, Irene Amelia, only child of William & Mary C., d. 1848, Dec. 29, a. 3 y. 3 m..
76. Ingraham, John L., d. 1846, Feb. 2, a. 67-9-6.
77. Ingraham, Mary Ann Drew, dau. of John L. & Anna, d. 1839, Dec. 5, a. 26-5-23.
78. Ingraham, Sarah Ann, dau. of Elizabeth, d. 1841, Sep. 14, a. 24 y. 15 d.
79. Ingraham, William, d. 1853, Dec. 29, in 35th y.
80. Johnston, Francis M., s. of Aleander & Phebe, d. 1862, Feb. 20, a. 10 m. 13 d.
81. Johnston, Ida C., dau. of Alexander & Phebe, d. 1858, Nov. 28, a. 3-7-25.
82. Johnston, William M., s. of Alexander & Phebe, d. 1863, Sep. 2, a. 2-5-25.
83. Jones, Nathan M., d. (1850?), (broken), a. 77-4-12.
84. Jones, Susan, w. of Nathan, d. 1869, Dec. 28, a. 79-4-8.
85. Koonz, Elizabeth, w. of Peter, d. 1866, May 3, a. 69 y.
86. Koonz, Peter, d. 1873, Apr. 18, in 79th y.
87. Lake, Hellin, w. of Stephen, d. 1845, Nov, 1, a. 32 y.
88. Lake, Maria, w. of John, d. 1842, June 28, in 42d y.
89. (Law) Mary Rice, w. of William, d. 1851, Feb. 23, a. 56-4-22.

90. Lester, George N., d. 1843, Feb. 11, a. 9-9-20.
91. Lewis, Maria L., dau. of Thomas & Mary J., d. 1861, May 13, a. 4-3-28.
92. Lewis, William T., Co. I, 128th N. Y. Vols., d. 1891, Mar. 18, a. 54 y.
93. Lucas, Arabella, only dau. of George & Sarah A., d. 1864, Aug. 16, a. 16 y.
94. McFarlin, Alfred, s. of Stephen & Phebe, d. 1859, Oct. 28, a. 33 y. 5 m.
95. McFarland, Elizabeth Cornwell, w. of Levi, b. 1803, May 8, d. 1885, Mar. 13.
96. McFarlin, Isaac C., s, of Levi & Elizabeth, d. 1839, Apr. 4, a. 11 m. 8 d.
97. McFarland, Levi, d. 1872, Mar. 18, in 65th y.
98. McIntosh, Johnnie, d. 1871, Jan. 24, in 24th y.
99. Marshall, Eli, d. 1866, Feb. 11, a. 63-4-22.
100. Marshall, Harriet, dau. of Eli & Catharine, d. 1858, Oct. 13, a. 16-2-24.
101. Marshall, Sarah, dau. of Eli & Catharine, d. 1858, Feb. 9, a. 26-3-28.
102. Mastin, Clara A. T.. dau. of David & Mary E., d. 1875, Jan. 11, a. 3 y.
103. Masten, Hezekiah G., Co. D, 128th N. Y. Vols., d. 1865, July 28, a. 25 y.
104. Masten, James E., d. 1879, May 5, in 39th y.
105. Moore, Maria, d. 1873, Jan. 27, a. 90 y.
106. Morris, Martha E., dau. of John & Mary L., d. 1850, May 24, a. 3 wks.
107. (Morris?), Rodah E., d. 1841, Apr. 22, a. 2 y.
108. Mo(wies), William P., d. 1892, July 12, a. 45 y. 14 d.
109. Newcomb, John, d. 1827, Feb. 6, a. 56-11-13.
110. Newcomb, Ruth, w. of John, d. 1834, Dec. 17, a. 62 y. 5 m.
111. Oakley, Eliza, w. of William M., d. 1866, Apr. 2, in 66th y.
112. Oakley, William M., d. 1875, Jan. 20, in 74th y.
113. Odell, Almira A. Baker, w. of Samuel D., d, 1858, Nov. 27, a. 36 y. 7 m.
114. Odell, Cornelia, dau. of Samuel D. & Almira, d. 1866, Aug. 18, a. 8-4-19.
115. Odell, Frances D., dau, of Milton & Harriett, d. 1855, Feb. 25, a. 5 m. 5 d.
116. Overocker, Sarah Lake, w. of Abraham L., d. 1865, Apr. 13, in 83d y.
117. Palmatier, Charles H., d. 1882, Feb. 3, a. 50 y.
118. Patten, Mary F., dau. of William T. & Sarah A., d. 1858, Mar. 27, a. 9-11-4.
119. Place, Louisa Matilda, dau. of Welcome & Louisa, d. 1853, Nov. 26, (age not decipherable).
120. Race, Maria Jane, d. 1866, Aug. 3, a. 2 y. 2 m.
121. Race, Phebe J. Stormes, w of Philo, 1831-1909.
122. Race, Philo, d. 1888, Nov. 1, a. 64 y. 5 m.
123. Rice, Alida, dau. of Jacob & Delia M., d. 1880, Mar. 25, a. 21 y. 6 m.
124. Rice, Egbert N., s. of Jacob & Delia, d. 1876, Mar. 16, a. 21-1-22.
125. Rice, Garrison, s. of Solomon & Sarah, d. 1843, Jan. 8, a. 5-10-5.
126. Rice, Mary Ann, w. of Jacob, d. 1849, Nov. 11, a. 44-6-10.
127. Robertson, Mary, b. 1813, June 12, d. 1884, Nov. 14.
128. Robertson, Richard T., d. 1863, May 26, a. 70-9-19.

129. Rogers, Alexander, Co. I, 150th N. Y. Vols., d. 1873, June 10, a. 42 y.
130. Rogers, Catherine, w. of Alexander, d. 1864, Sep. 21, a. 29 y. 5 m.
131. Rozell, Hannah, w. of William J., d. 1877, Apr. 18, in 73d y.
132. Shaw, Rachel, w. of Elymus, d. 1858, Apr. 9, a. 59-5-13.
133. Silvernail, John Henry, only s. of George & Sarah, d. 1844, June 18, a. 11-10-27.
134. Sleight, Martha, w. of Solomon, d. 1839, Mar. 29, a. 47 y.
135. Sleight, Solomon, d. 1843, Mar. 1, a. 70-3-10.
136. Smith, Aaron H., s. of William S. & Loretta, d. 1864, May 22, a. 1-5-22.
137. Spencer, Jane, w. of J. C., d. 1872, Sep. 13, in 71st y.
138. Stevens, Mary, dau, of Elijah & Mary, d. 1841, Feb. 16, a. 32 y.
139. Stewert, Anna, dau. of Thomas & Sarah, d. 1849, Jan. 13, in 73d y.
140. Stewart, Phebe, wid. of Josiah, d. 1843, Feb. 2, a. 51 y.
141. Stiwell, Daniel, d. 1844, Dec. 21, a. 55-3-27.
142. Stiwell, James Edward, d. 1852, Dec.12, a. 26-10-6.
143. Stilwell, John, d. 1837, Apr. 22, a. 77 y. 2 m.
144. Stilwell, Lydia, w. of Daniel, d. 1855, Oct. 27, a. 64-11-27.
145. Stillwell, Rebecca, d. 1843, Apr. 24, a. 75 y.
146. Storm, Catharine, w. of Jacob, d. 1875, Oct. 11, a. 66-6-18.
147. Storm, Jacob, d. 1867, Sep. 11, a. 64-5-28.
148. Storm, Joseph F., s. of Jacob & Catharine, d. 1862, Dec. 1, a. 9-2-5.
149. Storm, Luman, s. of Jacob & Catharine, d. 1855, Mar. 3, a. 4-5-15.
150. Storm, Rebecca, dau. of Jacob & Catharine, d. 1870, Sep.17, a. 31-8-21.
151. Storm, Susan Ann, dau. of Jacob & Catharine. d. 1855, Dec. 6, a. 23 y. 2 m.
152. Stormes, Abram, d. 1882, Nov. 15, in 76th y.
153. Stormes, Elizabeth Tripp, w. of Abram, d. 1879, Aug. 22, in 72d y.
154. Stormes, Kesiah Lake, w. of Jacob, d. 1871, July 16, a. 92-5-6.
155. Stormes, Matilda, dau. of Jacob & Kesiab, 1822-1891.
156. Storms, Catharine H., w. of John I., d. 184(0), Oct. 27. a. 40-3-27.
157. Storms, Catharine M., dau. of John I. & Catharine H., d. 186(2). Dec. 22, a. (21)-6-13.
158. Storms, John I., d. 1866, July 13, a. 69-7-26.
159. Storms, Phebe Jane, w. of Isaac, d. 1856, Apr. 5, a. 36 y. 1 m.
160. Taylor, Edward C., d. 1825, Nov. 15, a. 40 y.
161. Taylor, Maria C., w. of Edward C., d. 1831, July 10, a. 43 y.
162. Temple, Hester, w. of Aleander, d. 1833, Sep. 16, a. 35 y.
163. Thompson, John, d. 1881, May 2, a. 74 y.
164. Traver, Mary, w. of William L., d, 1845, Aug. 1, a. 38 y. 10 m.
165. Traver, William L., d. 1872, June 13, a. 71 y. 28 d.
166. Tripp, Elisha, d. 1844, Nov. 6, a. 30-4-8.
167. Turner, Abram T., d. 1865, Mar. 29, a. 33 y. 10 m,

168. Turner, George W., s. of John W. & Mary A., d. 1867, Feb. 6. a. 1 y. 9 m.
169. Wesley, Charlotte, dau. of John W. & Charlotte A., d. 1848, Oct. 2, a. 10-3-20.
170. Wesley, Mary E., dau. of John W. & Charlotte A., d. 1848, Oct. 13, a. 14-4-6.
171. Whitney, A., d. 1833, Mar. 5, (slate stone, nothing more decipherable).
172. Williams, Maria, w. of Peter, d. 1868, Sep. 10, a. 35 y. 5 m.
173. Williams, Peter, d. 1856, Feb .27, a. 41-6-4.
174. Wolf, Margaret, w. of Henry, d. 1848, Feb. 24, a. 53 y.

Miscellaneous

175. (?), Mary Nellie, d. 1875, Aug. 25, a. 9 m. 20 d.

Copied by Charlotte Carey Dingee (CCDingee@aol.com) and transcribed and submitted by Liz DuBois (ddubois@sinclair.net)

http://www.rootsweb.ancestry.com/~nydutche/cems/friendpv.htm

Interments in the FRIENDS' GROUND

"Old Gravestones of Dutchess County, New York" by J. W. Poucher published in 1924, pages 221-223.

Note: Some of Poucher's listings have been found to be inaccurate, so use these with caution. If you find any inaccuracies in this listing please send them to me so that I may correct them. Lynn Brandvold (lynnb@nmt.edu) Thanks.

CLASSIFICATION: Friends' burying ground.
LOCATION: Friends' meeting house, village of Pleasant Valley.
CONDITION: In good order.
INSCRIPTIONS: 133 in number. Copied July 1 and 2, 1914, by J. W. Poucher, M. D., and Mrs Poucher.
REMARKS: The Friends' meeting at Pleasant Valley was organized in 1802. The meeting is now extinct.

1. Attwood, Elijah, b. 1811, Apr. 20, d. 1841, Feb. 21.
2. Attwood, Jane T., dau. of William & Maria Thorn, d. 1843, Nov. 13, a. 28 y. 1 m.
3. Attwood, Maria Olivia, dau. of Elijah & Jane, b. 1840, May ---, d. 1841, Dec. 27.
4. Barber, Arselia, G., d. 1851, Oct. 9, a. 8-3-6.
5. Barber, Charles E., d. 1851, Sep. 25, a. 11 y. 7 m.
6. Barber, Sarah R., b. 1812, Sep. 1, d. 1890, Sep. 25.
7. Baright, Amy C., w. of Elijah, d. 1879, Dec. 30, a. 80-11-13.
8. Baright, Elijah, d. "6th m., 19th d., 1874," a. 71-2-20.
9. Baright, Elizabeth, dau. of Elijah & Amy (C.), d. "9th m., 16th, 1852," a. 21-10-20.
10. Barrett, Jane Ann Hart, w. of Lewis, 1826-1907.
11. Barrett, Lewis, 1827-1907.
12. Bloodgood, S. M., dau. of Daniel, d. 1837, Aug. 10.
13. Brown, Daniel, d. 1841, Sep. 30, a. 56-11-15.
14. Brown, George M., d. "8 m. 4, 1843," a. 19-1-11.
15. Brown, Seneca, d. "1 m. 5, 1819," a. 18-5-21.

16. Carpenter, Henry, d. "8 m. 22, 1851," a. 73 y.
17. Clearwater, Jeremiah, d. 1889, July 26, a. 91-3-14.
18. Clearwater, Timothy F., b. 1833, Mar. 29, d. 1873, Sep. 23.
19. Clearwater, Weltha, w. of Jeremiah, d. 1897, Oct. 1, in 93d y.
20. Cooley, James, a. 4 d.
21. Cooley, John, d. "5th m. 19th, 1856", a. 58 y.
22. Dean, Ann, d. 1836.
23. Dean, G. C. L., d. 1829.
24. Dean, Hannah B., d. "1 m. 9, 1860," a. 61 y.
25. Dean, Jonathan, b. "3 m. 27 d. 1747," d. "2 m. 16 d. 1813".
26. Dean, Julia, w. of Edwin, a. 28 y.
27. Dean, Mary, b. "3 in. 17 d. 1745," d. "9 m. 19 d. 1829".
28. Dean, Mary, d. "4 in 21 186(0)," a. 66 y.
29. DeGarmo, Edmund, d. "6th m. 28th, 1870," a. 48-8-8.
30. DeGarmo, Mary D., b, 1822, July 27, d. 1875, May 12.
31. Devine, Abram, 1831-1905.
32. Devine, Irving, s. of Reuben C. & Mary E., d. 1880, Nov. 10, a. 10 y. 8 m.
33. Devine, Reuben C.. 1840, Aug. 1, 1898, Aug. 27.
34. Divine, Phebe W. Drake, w. of Abraham, b. 1822, Feb. 4, d. 1881, Jan. 23.
35. Donaldson, Annie E. Downing. w. of Isaac T., 1838-1897.
36. Donaldson, Isaac T., 1831-1912.
37. Downing, Andrew S., b. "11th m. 12th, 1827," d. "7th m. 5th, 1894."
38. Downing, Coe S., b. "9th m. 17th, 1831," d. "8th m. 1st, 1876."
39. Downing, Emily, d. 1850, Oct. 2, a. 15-3-19.
40. Downing, Emma Ann McCord, w. of George, d. 1880, Apr. 14, a. 68 y.
41. Downing, Eliza, w. of Townsend, d. 1865, Dec. 11, a. 50-5-10.
42. Downing, George S., d. 1872, Dec. 11, a. 72 y.
43. Downing, Gideon W., b. "10th m. 1st, 1798," d. "2d m. 15th, 1864."
44. Downing, Judith Skidmore, w. of Gideon W., b. "3d m. 22d, 1801," d. "4th m. 3d, 1854."
45. Downing, Mary Ann, b. "1st of 11th m., 1803," d. "1st of 7th m., 1873," a. 69 y. 4 m.
46. Downing, Moses, d. "10th m. 19, 1853," a. 87 y. 1 m.
47. Downing, Sally Ann, b. "23 d of 2d m., 1806." d. "21 of 9th m., 1875," a. 69-6-2.
48. Downing, Susan Ann, b. "7th m. 22d, 1837," d. "3d m. 13th, 1854."
49. Downing, Townsend, b. "8 m. 3d, 1809," d. "12th m. 5th, 1879."
50. Drake, Augustus S., 1. "8-31-1852," a. 55 y.
51. Farrington, Eliza Ann, d. "11 m. 17 d. 1837," a. 28 y.
52. Farrington, Eunice, w of Timothy, d. "2 m. 18, 1841," a. 66-1-27.
53. Farrington, Mary, d. 1876, Jan. 19, a. 78 y. 6 m.
54. Farrington, children of George & Mary K.;

Elizabeth, d. 1828, Feb. 10, a. 2-3-7.
William H., d. 1829, Mar. 4, a. 1-3-4.
55. Fish, Elizabeth, w. of Ira, d. 1849, Mar. 11, a. 72 y. 5 m.
56. Fish, Ira, d. 1858, Feb. 14, a. 64-11-14.
57. Flagler, Anna, w. of John L., d. "26th of 4th m., 1857," a. 83 y.
58. Flagler, Benjamin, d. 1877, Feb. 5, a.. 81-2-12.
59. Flagler, Hannah Farrington, wid. of Silas, d. 1889, Aug. 17, a. 72 y. 10 m.
60. Flagler, Mary Strait, w. of Enoch, b. 1832, May 20, d. 1894, Dec. 7.
61. Gager, Hannah M. Velie, wid. of Joseph, d. 1896, Aug. 21, a. 86-6-7.
62. Gager, Robert, d. 1852, Nov. 18, a. (illegible).
63. Ganse, Winnie May, dau. of DeWitt T. & Mary, d. 1880, May 25, a. 10 m. 1 d.
64. Giddings, Charles L., b. 1849, Aug. 21, d. 1893, Oct. 10.
65. Giddings, Mary C., w. of N. L., d. 1885, June 16.
66. Green, Griffin, b. "3d m. 4th, 1786," d. "7th m. 31,1869."
67. Green, Mary, w. of Griffin, d. "8th m. 20th, 1852," a. 59-8-20.
68. Gurney, Amy, w. of David, d. 1812, Nov. 18, a. 17-8-6.
69. Gurney, Mary Ann, w. of William H., d. 1815, Mar. 7, a. 21-8-25.
70. Hastings, Eunice Jane, w. of John, b. 1820, Jan. 21, d. 1887, Oct. 15.
71. Hastings, Hannah, dau. of John & Jane, d. 1862, Aug. 4, a. 17 y. 5 m.
72. Hastings, John, b. 1805, Nov. 2, d. 1872, Dec. 11.
73. Hastings, William, s. of John & Jane, d. 1865, Nov. 14, a. 24 y. 3 m.
74. Hauxhurst, Catharine B., d. "5th m. 27, 1871," a. 72 y.
75. Hauxhurst, Deborah A., (dates sunken below ground).
76. Hauxhurst, Hannah, d. "3d m. 31, 1881".
77. Hauxhurst, Maria, d. 1880, June 19, a. 80 y.
78. Hauxhurst, Martha, d. "2d m. 6th, 1867," a. 76 y.
79. Hicks, Jerusha N., w. of Samuel, b. 1808, Nov. 21, d. 1886, Mar. 9.
80. Hicks, Samuel S., b. 1795, Dec. 3, d. 1869, Mar. 31.
81. Holmes, Phebe M., w. of George, d. 1844, Dec. 23, a. 28-8-21.
82. Howland, Seneca, d. "12th m. 25th, 1856," a. 81-6-25.
83. Ingraham, John C., d. 1889, July 5, a. 76 y., "Father."
84. Ingraham, Mary B., d. 1892, Oct. 10, a. 72 y., "Mother."
85. Knickerbocker, David H., s. of John & Sarah B., d. "9th m. 11, 1859," a. 15 y. 20 d.
86. Knickerbocker, Jane E., dau. of John & Sarah B., d. "11 m. 25, 1850," a. 19 y. 20 d.
87. Knickerbocker, John, d. "8th m, 18th, 1892," a. 85-1-6.
88. Knickerbocker, Martha, dau. of John & Sarah B., d. "11 m. 12th, 1847," a. 1-1-17.
89. Knickerbocker, Martha Alma, dau. of John & Sarah B., d. "9 m. 23d, 1850," a. 10 m. 11 d.

90. Knickerbocker, Sarah B. Sleight, w. of John, d. "10th m. 8th, 1875, a. 69-7-8.
91. Landis, Abbie Jane, w. of Samuel J., & dau. of Homer J. & Amittai W. Leach, b. 1837, Apr. 6, d. 1905, Nov. 26.
92. Lawton, Anthony, d. "8 m. Aug. 23, 1832," a. 41-10-15.
93. Leach, Amittai, w. of Homer J. & dau. of John & Grace Wanzer, b. 1805, Aug. 1, d.1876, Jan. 30.
94. Leach, Daniel Francis, s. of Homer J. & Amittai W., b. 1830, Jan. 28, d. 1881, Oct. 16.
95. Leach, Homer J., b. 1800, Oct. 15, d. 1867, Oct. 18.
96. Masten, Charles, d. 1859. Sep. 15, a. 54 y. 10 (m).
97. Masten, Elmira Lake, w. of Charles, d. 1878, Aug. 24, a. 69-4-8.
98. Masten, John V., d. 1879, Aug. 30, a. 46-5-17.
99. Masten, William H., d. 1802, Aug. 26, a. 29-10-29.
100. McCord, Catharine, d. 1872, Aug. 1, a. 55 y.
101. McCord, Elizabeth H., d. "10th m. 10, 1865," a. 69-4-5.
102. McCord, Sarah H., d. 1849, Aug. 19, a. 76-1-25.
103. Miller, Elizabeth Noe. w. of William B., d. 1852, Apr. 5, a. 28-3-18.
104. Palmer, Gulielma, d. "3d m. 21st, 1878," a. 71-5-17.
105. Palmer, James, d. "5th m. 13th, 1893," in 82d y.
106. Palmer, Jesse, d. "2d m. 1st, 1883," a. 74 y. 7 d.
107. Palmer, Peter, b. "1 m. 8th, 1808," d. "4th m. 4th, 1889."
108. Sleight, Elizabeth Barnes, w. of John, d. "10th m. 2d. 1853," a. 76-3-18.
109. Strait, George S., b. 1834, Apr. 3, d. 1875, Feb. 8.
110. Strait, Phebe Farrington, w. of Justus, b. 1803, Feb. 11, d. 1868, Mar 5.
111. Stringham, George J., s. of Willet & Eliza, d. "11 m. 15, 1853, a. 10 m.
112. Stringham, Owen D., d. 1852.
113. Stringham, Sarah, d. 1889, Mar. 15, a. 64 y.
114. Stringham, Susan A., d. "30th of 9th m., 1867," in 47th y.
115. Thorn, Ann W., d. 1826, Dec. 31, a 12 y.
116. Thorn, Edwin, s. of William & Maria, d. 1825, Mar. 5, a. 15 y. 3 m.
117. Thorn, Jane, w. of Edgar, & dau. of J. M. Thorn, d. 1828, June 2, a. 25 y. (Note: Thorn has been crossed out in pen and 'Thurston' typed at the end of the line.)
118. Thorn, Joseph, d. 1860, Dec. 21, a. 82-6-5.
119. Thorn, Lydia L., w. of Joseph, d. "29th of 8th m., 1863," in 76th y.
120. Thorn, Maria, w. of William, b. 1781, Feb. 15, d. 1845, Jan. 17.
121. Thorn, Mary S., dau. of Edgar & Eliza Ann, d. 1812, Jan. 8, a. 6 d.
122. Thorn, Priscilla, d. 1832, Mar. 16, a. 15 y.
123. Thorn, Samuel, d. 1809, Mar. 15, a. 6 y.
124. Thorn, Sarah, w. of Joseph, d. 1827, Jan. 8, a. 47 y
125. Thorn, Sarah H., d. 1840, Mar. 6, in 28th y.

126. Thorn, William, s. of William & Jemima, b. "1 m. 21, 1781," d. "11 m., 6, 1869," a. 88-9-15.
127. Tompkins, John B., 1839, Feb. 5, --- 1913, Mar. 18.
Sarah E. Downing, his wife, 1839, June 30, --- 1903, Oct. 29.
128. Townsend, Betsey T., w. of George, b. "6th m. 27th, 1802." d. "4th m. 18th, 1869".
129. Townsend, Sarah, w. of Thomas. d. "12 m. 13, 1836," a. 23-11-19.
130. Townsend, Thomas, d. "1 m. 12, 1839," a. 25-3-17.
131. Vail, Jarvis, d. 1859, Nov. 4, a. 61 y. 3 d.
132. Vail, Lydia, d. "10 m. Oct. 18, 1842," a. 41-1-10.
133. Welling, Delilah, d. 1861, Feb. ---, a. 67 y.

Copied by Charlotte Carey Dingee (CCDingee@aol.com) and transcribed and submitted by Liz DuBois (ddubois@sinclair.net)

Reg.	First		Last	Rank	Co.	Age	Enlisted	Term	Pd	Notes
128	George	F.	Abbott				Aug-1864	1 yr	$300	
150	Smith	P.	Allen	Pvt	C	19	Oct-1862	3 yrs	$200	Died
128	Charles		Baker				Aug-1862	3 yrs	$300	(TC) lists 16th Art.
128	William	C.	Bartlett		A	21	Sep-1862			
	J	F	Bevits							Name appears in Smith book only
128	Bartlett	H.	Bishop				Aug-1862	3 yrs	$0	
	Storms		Bishop						$0	
150	John	C.	Bradley	Pvt.	C	19	Sep-1862	3 yrs	$300	(TC) lists 16th Art, E: Jan-1864
20	William	H.	Branne				Jan-1863	3 yrs	$300	(TC) Listed as "colored"
150	John		Brennan				Sep-1862	3 yrs	$150	(TC) lists 16th Art, E: Jan-1864
128	Michael		Brennan				Jan-1865	1 yr	$320	
128	Christopher		Brier	2ndCPl	D		Sep-1862			Promoted to Sgt., Sp. fix & rank fr. Hanaburgh
128	Thomas		Bullis		A	44	Sep-1862			
150	Charles		Burdick, Jr.	Pvt.	F	18				Buried in 1st Pres. Ch. PV
150	Benjamin	S.	Burroughs	Pvt.	A	29	Sep-1862	3 yrs	$200	
150	Christopher		Burt				Sep-1862	3 yrs	$200	
150	Thomas	J.	Burt	Cpl.	K	36				

128	James		Burt					3 yrs	$50	
150	G.	J.	Burts				Oct-1862	3 yrs	$200	
150	George	S.	Cady	Pvt.	C	21	Aug-1864	1 yr	$0	
128	John		Cass		A	20	Sep-1862			
150	Edmund		Cody	Pvt.	C.	28	Sep-1862			Buried in S. Pauls Epis. Chchyd, PV
128	James		Carlow		A	45	Sep-1862			
150	William	H	Cary					3 yrs	$200	
1 Art	Thomas		Casey				Jan-1865	1 yr	$300	
	Amos								$0	
128	William		Chamberlain		A	38	Sep-1862			
121	Allen	S.	Clark				Jan-1865		$300	
128	John		Coller		A	38	Sep-1862			
	John		Corumph				Oct-1862	3 yrs	$200	
80	Riley		Crocker				Nov-1862	3 yrs	$200	(TC) lists Reg. as 150
	Charles	E.	Dennis				Dec-1862	3 yrs	$50	
	John		Donnelly						$0	
16th	Philips		Duncan				Jan-1863	3 yrs	$300	
16th	Spencer		Duncan				Jan-1864	3 yrs	$300	
150	George		Emmerson					3 yrs	$150	
150	Peter	H.	Fanander	Pvt.	I	41	Jan-1865	1 yr		Txfer to Co D, 6th Inf 8-Jun-1865
150	Thomas		Fitzgibbons	Pvt.	H	24				
150	Charles	E.	Florence	Pvt.	C	18	Sep-1862	3 yrs	$200	Buried in

										Washington Hollow
150	Edward	L.	Florence	Cpl.	I	19				Buried in Washington Hollow
128	Matthew		Foster		D		Sep-1862	3 yrs	$0	Prisoner- per David Hanaburgh
150	Peter	H.	Furrenden	Pvt.	unk.	41	Jan-1865	1 yr	$300	
	William		Genet				Oct-1862	3 yrs	$200	
150	Frederick		Gerard					3 yrs	$200	
159	James		Gibbons					3 yrs	$150	
150	Thomas	F.	Gibbons					3 yrs	$200	
150	Frederick		Giraud	Cpl.	C	25	Sep-1862	3 yrs		
128	S.		Glensal						$50	
46	Herman		Goodeck				Jan-1865	1 yr	$350	
20	Nelson		Gray				Feb-1864	3 yrs	$300	(TC) Listed as "colored"
16th	Isaac		Green				Jan-1864	3 yrs	$300	
159	John	L	Haight				Oct-1862	3 yrs	$200	(TC) shows 167 Reg.
106	John		Hammond				Jan-1865	1 yr	$400	
112	Richard	R.	Hawkins				Jan-1865	1 yr	$300	
	Peter	G.	Hemlett							Promoted Hosp. Steward, June 9, 1864
	James		Hill						$0	
150	Edmund		Horton	Pvt.	A	34				Buried 1st Presby. Chchyd. PV

150	Nathaniel		Horton				Aug-1864	1 yr	$300	
159	Collins		Jackson				Oct-1862	3 yrs	$200	
150	Jim		James				Aug-1864	1 yr	$300	
128	Thomas		Jones				Jul-1862	3 yrs	$200	(TC) shows Reg. as 150 & E 21-Oct-1862, comm. 1st Lt in 3rd Reg. Eng. Corp.
150	William		Jones	Pvt.	C	34		3 yrs	$200	
150	Henry	L	Jones				Oct-1862	3 yrs	$200	
21	Benjamin		Jones				Aug-1864	1 yr	$300	hand written " 21st Artillery"
	William		Jones				Aug-1862	3 yrs		
150	James		Kerr	Pvt.	K	32	Aug-1864	1 yr		
80	Daniel		Kipp				Jun-1865	1 yr	$300	
16 Art.	William		Knowlton				Oct-1863	3 yrs	$300	
	Christopher		Laberas						$0	
16 Art.	James	O.	Lake				Dec-1863	3yrs	$300	
	Lewis		Lawrence					3 yrs	$100	
8 Art.	William	E.	Lawrence				Feb-1864	3 yrs	$300	
128	James	A.	Leary				Dec-1863	3 yrs		Died on furlough in NY & name sp. - Hanaburgh (Dec

										15,1863)
150	Isaac		Leray				Oct-1862	3 yrs	$50	
16 Art.	James		Leray				Oct-1863	3 yrs	$300	
	Joseph	E.	Lockwood						$0	(TC) list only, enlisted as Cpl
176	John		Lockwood				Nov-1862	9 mo	$200	(TC) show 176 NY Inf., enlisted as Cpl
150	Theodore		Lockwood	Cpl.	I	18	Sep-1862	3 yrs	$200	Enlisted as Cpl
	Andrew	J.	Mackey						$0	(TC) list only
128	William	H	Mackey				Aug-1862	3 yrs	$50	Prisoner , sp McKay-per David Hanaburgh
150	Patrick		Mangin				Oct-1862	3 yrs	$200	
150	Rowland		Marshall				Sep-1862	3 yrs	$200	Died @ Georgetown, Sep 1863
128	John	J.	Marshall				Aug-1862	3 yrs		Disabled
1 Art.	William		Martin				Jun-1865	1 yr	$350	
3	David		Mastin				Mar-1865	1 yr	$0	
61	James	E.	Mastin				Feb-1865	1 yr	$0	
62	Charles	Henry	Mastin				Aug-1861	3 yrs	$0	Battle of Gettysburg, Fredericksburg with Grant.
47	John	Hart	Mastin				Aug-1861	3 yrs	$0	Prisoner- per David

Art.										Hanaburgh
150	James	E.	Mastin				Feb, 1865	3 yrs	$200	
61	George	L.	Mastin				Feb-1864	3 yrs	$300	
150	Walter		Mastin				Aug-1864	1 yr	$300	
150	Walter	P.	Mastin				Aug-1864	1 yr	$600	Died at Ft. Schyyler
42	Edward		Matthews				Jan-1865	1 yr	$400	
	John		McCord				Jan-1864	3 yrs	$300	Illegible
150	William	H	McFarlin	Cpl.	C	27	Oct-1862	3 yrs	$200	Taken prisoner after taking 18 battles, died in Salisbury prison
128	William	H	McKay		D		Sep-1862			Wagoner, captured Oct 19,1864 (PV Historical notes)
	William		McMachin							
91	Samuel		McMackan				Jan-1865	1 yr	$425	
150	Horace		Millard	Pvt.	C	45	Oct-1862	3 yrs	$200	
150	Jacob	F.	Miller	Pvt.	H	44	Sep-1862	1 yr	$400	to Vet. Res. after enlistment
150	Leonard		Mitchell				Oct-1862	3 yrs	$200	
150	David		Moon	Pvt.	C	23				
106	Charles		Moore				Jun-1865	1 yr	$300	
	Harrison		Moore						$0	(TC) roster only
150	David		Mowers					3 yrs	$200	
150	James		Murphy				Sep-1862	3 yrs	$200	Died at Tallahassee

	Thomas		Murrey					3 yrs	$150	
	Alfred	W.	Noble						$0	(TC) roster only
128	William	H	Oakley		C	28	Sep-1862			
159	Archibald		Ostram					3 yrs	$200	
128	Walter		Palmatier		D		Sep-1862	3 yrs	$0	
150	William		Palmatier	Cpl.	C	28	Oct-1862	3 yrs	$200	Died in battle
	John		Parke							
150	Charles		Pells	Pvt.	C	46	Sep-1862	3 yrs	$200	
16 Art.	George		Peters				Sep-1863	3 yrs	$0	Promoted to Hosp. Stewart Jan 9, 1864
150	Henry		Peters	Pvt.	C	18	Aug-1863	3 yrs	$0	(TC) lists 16 Art, listed on Reg. roster of 150
150	William	B.	Place				Sep-1862	3 yrs	$200	
150	Aaron	N	Plain				Oct-1862	3 yrs	$200	
128	Daniel	B.	Ryder		D		Sep-1862	3 yrs	$50	Wounded May 27, 1863 at Port Hudson, died at Baton Rouge. sp Ryder - Hanaburgh & PV notes
80	Martin	L.	Riggs				Jun-1865	1 yr	$300	
	James		Rue							
150	Lawrence		Russell				Oct-1862	3 yrs	$200	
150	Matthew		Shaffer	Pvt.	E	26				
150	Matthew		Shelborne				Jan-1865	1 yr	$300	

150	John		Silvernail				Oct-1862	3 yrs	$200	
20	John	A.	Simmons				Dec-1863	3 yrs	$300	(TC) listed as "colored"
128	Abraham	T	Smith		D					Captured 1884, died at PV,Mar 23, 1885 (PV Historical Notes)
91	Charles		Smith				Jan-1865	1 yr	$300	
128	John	Henry	Smith		D		Aug-1862	3 yrs	$50	Died after Fort Hudson
62	Walter		Smith				Jul-1861	3 yrs	$0	Killed July 1863
128	William	P.	Smith					1 yr		Killed at Malvern Hill, July 1, 1863
150	Andrew		Spencer	Pvt.	C	34	Aug-1864	1 yr	$125	Buried in Pok. Rural Cemetery
16 Art.	John		Stewart				Dec-1863	3 yrs	$300	
16 Art.	Everett		Storms				Sep-1863	3 yrs	$0	
	Lewis		Storms						$0	
61	James		Storms				Feb-1864	3 yrs	$300	Ship wrecked March 31, 1865. (hard to read)
128	John		Taff		D		Aug-1862		$0	Enlisted as 2ndCpl,reg. , sp from David Hanaburgh & PV Hist. notes

	Charles		Tager				Jan-1865	1 yr	$350	
159	William		Talleman					3 yrs	$100	
	Howard		Tihen					3 yrs	$200	
16 Art.	John		Townsend				Dec-1863	3 yrs	$300	
128	Abram	T	Turner				Sep-1862	3 yrs	$0	Prisoner- per David Hanaburgh
	Oliver		Underhill					3 yrs	$50	
159	Edward		Vail				Oct-1862	3 yrs	$200	
95	Robert		Vance				Jan-1865	1 yr	$300	
16 Art.	Charles	E.	VanLock				Jan-1864	3 yrs	$300	
128	Benjamin	H	Vanwyck		D		Sep-1862		$0	Commissary servant (PV Hist list)
150	Allen	J	Velie	Pvt.	C	31	Oct-1862	3 yrs	$200	Txfer into 60th Inf.
16 Art.	Morris		Wagner				Oct-1863	3 yrs	$325	
128	William		Walker		D		Aug-1863	3 yrs	$50	Promoted to Cpl Nov 1, 1864.
16 Art.	Edward	S	Walters				Oct-1863	3 yrs	$300	Enlisted as musician
16 Art.	Edward		Waters				Dec-1863	3 yrs		
106	William		Webb				Jan-1865	1 yr	$300	
150	Jacob		Webber				Jan-1865	1 yr	$300	
150	John		Welch				Jan-1865	1 yr	$300	

20	Elijah		Weldon				Dec-1863	3 yrs	$300	(TC) Listed as "colored"
128	Seth		Wheeler		A	44	Oct-1862	3 yrs	$200	to Vet. Res. after enlistment
150	William	C	Wile	Pvt.	G	17	Oct-1862	3 yrs	$200	
	Charles	F	Wilkenson					3 yrs	$150	
150	Alfred		Williams	Cpl.	C	21	Oct-1862	3 yrs	$200	
	George		Williams				Feb-1864	3 yrs	$300	Regiment illegible
150	Henry	P	Williams	Pvt.	C	18	Sep-1862	3 yrs	$200	Wound thru his body and lived
150	John		Williams					3 yrs	$150	
159	Theodore		Williams				Oct-1862	3 yrs	$200	
	Thomas		Williams					3 yrs	$150	
106	William	C.	Williams				Jan-1865	1 yr	$300	
7 NY?	Edmund		Wolfew				Sep-1861	3 yrs	$0	Wounded at Williamsburgh,name sp & Reg. not clear
150	Joseph		Wooley	Cpl.	C	18	Sep-1862	3 yrs	$200	

Acknowledgements

Unless otherwise noted, all photos are from the files of the Pleasant Valley Historical Society.

Codes for photographers or contributors are:

Images from the George Greenwood files (GBG)
H. Maynard Johnson (HMJ)
Edna Hommel (EH)
Teddi Luzzi Southworth (TeddiS)
Terri Ghee (TerriG)
John Roosa (JohnR)
Pat Holt (PH)
Caroline Dolfi (CD)
Pat Beatty (PatB)
Barbara Shapley (BShapley)
Carl Tomik (PVSuperv)
Remo Valdetta (RV)

When I used historical information from the book "Sesquicentennial of the Post Office, Pleasant Valley, N. Y. 1813 - 1963" I kept the spirit of the writers words, and noted who the author was. I felt the perspective of these old timers of Pleasant Valley was important for the flavor of my book.

Netherwood Baptist history from page 27 by Edyth Budd

Saint Stanislaus Roman Catholic Church history from page 34 by Helen Reed (Mrs. John)

St. Paul's Church History from page 31 by Edyth Stott

Quaker history from page 29 by Edna Rossway (Mrs. J. Christopher)

Methodist Church history page 28 by Sara Nye & Ivy Johnson

Masonic history from page 40 by Emet Appel
Eastern Star information from page 47 by Sara E. Nye (Mrs. Almon O.)

American Legion Organizational information from page 45, by Homer Teal, Commander 1963

History of fire department pages 43 & 44 by Herb Oakley.

List of names on the Veterans Memorial from Carl Rennia
Quaker history also from Bulls Head Friends clerk Mary Cadbury

History of Library from_ GOLDEN ANNIVERSARY, 1903 – 1953, Pleasant Valley Free Library booklet.

Endnotes:

---

[a] Patent from Book 7, page 80-82 in series 12943, Letters Patent. NY State Archives 11A36 Cultural Education Center, Albany, NY 12230
[b] McDermott. 2004. page 179
[c] ibid. page 182
[d] Smith 1877. page 50
[e] Hasbrouck 1909. page 419
[f] ibid. page 421
[g] Rinaldi 1999. page 3, 4
[h] ibid. page 14
[i] ibid. page 16
[j] ibid. page 21
[k] I did not use dates because some were unclear, this is the best we could come up with for the sequence of supervisors
[l] From "This Is A Pleasant Valley, memories of Mrs. F. Irving (Irene) Bower written by Helen Myers, Sunday New Yorker Feature Writer, April 4 & 11, 1948.
[m] http://www.kinglyheirs.com/CNE/CNEPENorth.html
[n] History of Duchess County by James H. Smith 1882
[o] ibid., 145
[p] Poughkeepsie Daily Eagle, October 23, 1862, page 3
[q] Sesquicentennial of Post Office, page 7
[r] Sesquicentennial of Post Office, page 12, 13
[s] ibid, Hermena E. Plankenhorn, page 15
[t] Pleasant Valley Voice, Pleasant Valley, NY March 20, 1968, page 15
[u] Pleasant Valley Voice, Pleasant Valley, NY June 3, 1982, page 3
[v] http://pleasantvalleylibrary.org/ date June 11, 2012
[w] http://en.wikipedia.org/wiki/Ground_Observer_Corps
[x] http://www.afa.org/_private/Magazine/Feb2006/0206GOC.asp June 15, 2012
[y] http://www.westernmusic.com/performers/hof-robison.html#, http://en.wikipedia.org/wiki/Carson_Robison
[z] http://www.erh.noaa.gov/er/nerfc/historical/Sep1938.html
[aa] http://www.erh.noaa.gov/historical/aug1955.htm
[bb] Poughkeepsie New Yorker, Wednesday, June 5, 1957
[cc] http://fema.gov/news/disasters.fema?year=1973
[dd] Poughkeepsie Journal, Tuesday, April 17, 2007
[ee] Poughkeepsie Journal, Wednesday, April 18, 2007
[ff] http://www.fema.gov/news/disasters_state.fema?id=36
[gg] http://www.shekomeko.org/about-us.php
[hh] First Presbyterian Church, Pleasant Valley, NY, page 40
[ii] Ibid, pages 4-39
[jj] http:// www.pvpresby.org

Bibliography

Dyer, F. H. (1908). *A Compendium of the War of the Rebellion.* Des Moines, Ia.: Broadfoot Publishing Company, Morningside Press.
First Presbyterian church, Pleasant Valley, NY. (1965). This Earthen Vessel. Pleasant Valley, New York, United States of America.
Hanaburgh, D. (1894). *History of the One Hundred and Twenty-eighth Regiment: New York Volunteers (U.S.Infantry): in the Late Civil War.* Poughkeepsie, New York: Press of Enterprise Publishing.
Hasbrouck, F. (1909). The History of Dutchess County, New York. In F. Hasbrouck, *The History of Dutchess County, New York* (pp. 419-425). Poughkeepsie, NY: S.A.Matthieu.
J. H. Mather and L. P. Brockett, M. (1848). A Geographical History of the State of New York. In M. J. H. Mather and L. P. Brockett, *A Geographical History of the State o New York* (p. 191). Utica, NY: H. H. Hawley & Co.
King, C. D. History of education in Dutchess County. In C. D. King, *History of education in Dutchess County.*
MacCracken, H. N. (1956). Old Dutchess Forever! In H. N. MacCracken, *Old Dutchess Forever!* New York, NY: Hastings House.
McDermott, W. P. (2004). *Dutchess County's Plain Folks: Enduring Uncertainty, Inequality and Uneven Prosperity 1725-1875.* Clinton Corners, NY: Kerleen Press.
Reynolds, W. J. (1924). Old gravestones of Dutchess County, New York. In W. J. Poucher, *Old gravestones of Dutchess County, New York.* Poughkeepsie, NY.
Rinaldi, T. (1999). Pleasant Valley Manufactory. In T. Rinaldi, *Pleasant Valley Manufactory.* Pleasant Valley, NY: The Town of Pleasant Valley Historical Society.
Sesquicentennial of the Pleasant Valley Post Office. (1963, October 1). Pleasant Valey, New York, United States of American: Committee for The
Smith, J. H. (1882). *History of Duchess County.* Syracuse: D. Mason and Co.
Smith, P. H. (1877). *General History of Duchess County from 1609 to 1876.* Pawling, New York: the author.
Wilhelm, S. L. (1976, August 1). History and Hearsay, Pleasant Valley's First 200 Years. 1976, New York, United States of America: Mid-Hudson Library System.